ACCLAIM FOR **MICHAEL CONNELLY**'S

CRIME BEAT

"Engrossing. . . . Connelly's characters are carefully drawn, his eye for detail is sharp, and the crimes he explores are fascinating."
— John Keenan, *Omaha World-Herald*

"One of the fascinations of the collection is spotting the police-beat details — the fellow with teardrops tattooed below his eyes, the detective who chewed the earpiece of his glasses — that later punctuate the Harry Bosch novels. . . . *Crime Beat* will be of interest to close students of Connelly's fiction, to some journalists, and to anyone interested in how the sow's ear of fact becomes the silk purse of fiction."
— Patrick Anderson, *Washington Post*

"A remarkable compendium illustrating the flowering of a revered mystery writer."
— Rod Cockshutt, *Raleigh News & Observer*

"Connelly's reporting is good, clean, straightforward. . . . This is exactly the sort of subject that calls for hardheadedness, and Connelly supplies it, not in his prose but in his determination not to take the word of authority simply because it comes from authority."
— Charles Taylor, *New York Times Book Review*

"*Crime Beat* illustrates the art of solid police reporting. . . . The writing is lean and economical, unburdened by embellishments; yet this no-frills approach captures situations so perfectly."
— Oline H. Cogdill, *South Florida Sun-Sentinel*

"*Crime Beat* offers revealing insight into the formation of an author whose writing stands a cut above most of the genre fiction topping the bestseller list."
— Robin Vidimos, *Denver Post*

ALSO BY MICHAEL CONNELLY

The Black Echo

The Black Ice

The Concrete Blonde

The Last Coyote

The Poet

Trunk Music

Blood Work

Angels Flight

Void Moon

A Darkness More Than Night

City of Bones

Chasing the Dime

Lost Light

The Narrows

The Closers

The Lincoln Lawyer

Echo Park

The Overlook

CRIME BEAT

A DECADE OF COVERING COPS AND KILLERS

MICHAEL CONNELLY

BACK BAY BOOKS
LITTLE, BROWN AND COMPANY
NEW YORK   BOSTON   LONDON

Back Bay Books / Little, Brown and Company
Hachette Book Group USA
237 Park Avenue, New York, NY 10017
Visit our Web site at www.HachetteBookGroupUSA.com

Little, Brown and Company hardcover edition, May 2006
First Back Bay paperback edition, June 2007

Originally published as *Crime Beat: Selected Journalism 1984–1992*
in hardcover by Steven C. Vascik Publications, 2004

Permissions to reprint the stories begin on page 371.

Library of Congress Cataloging-in-Publication Data

Connelly, Michael.
    Crime beat : a decade of covering cops and killers / Michael Connelly.
        p.   cm
    ISBN 978-0-316-15377-5 (hc) / 978-0-316-01279-9 (pb)
    1. Crime — United States — Case studies.   2. Homicide investigation — United
States — Case studies.   3. Crime in mass media.   I. Title.
HV6783.C715   2006
363.25'95230973 — dc22   2005029074

10 9 8 7 6 5 4 3 2 1

Q-MART

Printed in the United States of America

Death is my beat. I make my living from it. I forge my professional reputation on it. I treat it with the passion and precision of an undertaker — somber and sympathetic about it when I'm with the bereaved, a skilled craftsman with it when I'm alone. I've always thought the secret of dealing with death was to keep it at arm's length. That's the rule. Don't let it breathe in your face.

— from *The Poet*

CONTENTS

PART TWO The Killers

PART THREE The Cases

CRIME BEAT

INTRODUCTION:

WATCHING THE DETECTIVES

MOMENTS. It all comes down to moments. I have been watching the detectives for more than thirty years. It all started because of a single moment. The best things that I have seen and taken into my imagination and then seeded into my fiction came to me in moments. Sometimes I am haunted by the what ifs. What if I hadn't looked out my car window that night when I was sixteen? What if I hadn't seen the detective take off his glasses? What if I had gone to L.A. for the first time a day later, or I hadn't answered the phone the time my editor called me to send me up the hill to check out a murder?

3

Let me try to explain. Let me try to tell you about a few of these moments.

When I was sixteen years old I worked as a night dishwasher in a hotel restaurant on the beach in Fort Lauderdale, Florida. The place stayed open late and the pots and pans that were used to cook in all day had to be soaked, scrubbed and cleaned. I often didn't get out of that place until late.

One night I was driving my Volkswagen Beetle home from work. The streets were almost deserted. I came to a red light and stopped the car. I was tired and just wanted to get home. There were no other cars at the intersection and no cars coming. Thinking about running the light, I checked both ways for cops and when I looked to my left I saw something.

A man was running. He was on the sidewalk, running full speed toward the beach, in the direction I had just come from. He was big and bearded with bushy hair down to his shoulders. He wasn't a jogger. He was running either to or from something. He wore blue jeans and a lumberjack shirt. He was wearing boots, not running shoes. Forgetting about the traffic light, I watched the man and saw him start to peel off his shirt as he ran, revealing a printed T-shirt underneath. He pulled the outer shirt off and then bundled it around something he had been clutching in his hand. Barely breaking his stride, he shoved the shirt into the interior branches of a hedge next to the sidewalk and then kept going.

I made a U-turn when the light changed. The running man was a few blocks ahead of me. I drove slowly, following and watching him. I saw him duck into the doorway of a bar called The Parrot. It was a bar I was familiar with. Not because I had ever been inside — I was too young. It was familiar because on numerous occasions I had noticed the line of motorcycles parked in front of it. I had seen the big men going in to do their drinking there. It was a place I was wary of.

I drove by The Parrot and made another U-turn. I went back to the hedge and parked my bug. I looked around, then quickly got out. At the hedge I stuck my hand into the branches and retrieved the bundled shirt. It felt heavy in my hands. I unwrapped it. There in the shirt was a gun.

A charge of fear and adrenaline went through me. I quickly rewrapped the gun and put it back in its place. I ran to my car and I drove away.

But then I stopped at a phone booth. When I reached my father and told him what I had just seen and done and discovered, he told me to come pick him up. He said we were going to call the police and go back to the hedge.

Fifteen minutes later my father and I were at the hedge when two police cars, with blue lights flashing from their roofs, pulled up. I told the officers what I had seen and what I had done. I led them to the gun. They told me there had been a robbery nearby. The victim had been shot in the head. They said the running man sounded like the guy they were looking for.

I spent the next four hours in the detective bureau. I was interviewed and reinterviewed by detectives, one in particular who was gruff and had a no-nonsense air about him. He told me that the victim might not make it, that I might end up being the only witness. Because of my description of the running man, several men with long hair, beards and printed T-shirts were pulled out of The Parrot and taken to the police department to stand in suspect lineups. I was the one looking through the one-way glass at them. I was the only witness. I had to pick the shooter.

There was only one problem. They didn't have the guy. It had been dark out but the street was lighted. I clearly saw the man who stashed the gun and knew they didn't have him. Sometime between when I saw him duck into The Parrot and when the police came to round up patrons fitting my description, the shooter had slipped away.

This did not sit well with the detectives. They believed they had the guy. They believed that I was simply too scared or intimidated to make the ID. I could not convince them and after going back and forth with the gruff detective for what seemed like hours it ended badly. My father demanded my release and I left the department with that detective thinking I had been too afraid to step up. I knew he was wrong but it didn't make me feel any better. Although I had been honest, I knew I had let him down.

I started reading the newspaper after that night. Religiously. At first it was to look for stories about the shooting. The victim survived, but I never heard from the detectives again and I wondered what had happened to the case. Was the shooter ever identified? Was he ever caught? I also became fascinated with the crime stories and the detectives working the cases. South Florida was a strange place. A torrent of drug money was flooding the coast. Fast boats and cars. Smugglers were moving into the best neighborhoods. Crimes of violence happened everywhere at any time. There seemed to always be a lot of crime stories to read.

I got hooked. Soon I was reading true-crime books and then crime novels. In the years that followed I discovered the work of Joseph Wambaugh and Raymond Chandler. And eventually I decided I wanted to be a writer. I wanted to work for a newspaper on the crime beat. I wanted to watch and learn about the detectives and then one day write about them in novels. All because of a moment, all because I had looked out my window.

MANY YEARS LATER I returned to the detective bureau where I had spent those hours and disappointed those detectives. When I returned it was as a reporter. I was on the police beat and I would visit the bureau almost daily, my assignment to chronicle the crimes of the city.

The gruff detective was still there. The years in between had sanded down his edges a little bit. At first I ignored him and he didn't remember me. Eventually, though, I told him who I was, reminded him of that night and once more made my case; that they didn't have the shooter, that the running man had gotten away. He still didn't believe me. He still believed I had been afraid that night to step up.

Over the course of a few years I was often in that detective bureau but I never won the detective over. It pained me but didn't deter me. In fact, it was in that detective bureau that the next important moment occurred.

It was a small thing but perhaps the single most important thing I ever saw as a crime writer. And it is recounted here in the first story of this collection.

After numerous requests and lengthy negotiations that went all the way up to the chief of police, I was granted complete access to the homicide squad for one week. Full access. I was given a pager and if the homicide squad got called out, then so would I. My assignment was to write about life in homicide, to get the inside look.

The irony of crime beat journalism — maybe all of journalism — is that the best stories are really the worst stories. The stories of calamity and tragedy are the stories that journalists live for. It gets the adrenaline churning in their blood and can burn them out young, but nevertheless it is a hard fact of the business. Their best day is your worst day.

This held true for my week with the homicide squad. It turned into a great story for me — but not for the three people who were murdered during the course of time I was riding with the squad.

The single story that influenced my writing more than any other came at the end of the week, in the last hour of my weeklong stay with the squad. I sat in the squad supervisor's office, going over the last-minute details and questions before I would turn my pager in and go back to the newspaper to write the story.

Sergeant George Hurt was tired — he and his detectives had chased three murders in five days. Sitting at his desk, he took off his glasses to rub his eyes. When he dropped the glasses on his desk I noticed that the earpiece had a deep groove cut into it. It was like spying a diamond in the sand, for I knew exactly how that groove had gotten there.

During the week I had watched the detectives at work, I had seen Sergeant Hurt take off his glasses on numerous occasions. Invariably, he hooked the earpiece in his mouth so his hands were free. At the murder scenes I had seen him approach the victim's body and take his glasses off, always hooking them in his mouth. These were solemn moments. He was observing the victim as a detective but there seemed to be something else going on as well. A sort of communion, or secret promise. It was not something he would talk to me about when I asked.

But now I saw the earpiece and I knew something. I knew that when he hooked his glasses in his mouth, his teeth clenched so tightly on them that they cut into the hard plastic of the earpiece. It said something about the man, about the job, about the world. It was a telling detail that opened up a window into this man's life. It said all that needed to be said about his dedication, motivation and relationship to his job. It was the most important thing I had seen in a week of seeing things I knew were important and vital to me.

I instinctively knew that as a writer I had to look for this. From now on I had to find the telling detail in all the people I wrote about, whether it was a crime story for a newspaper or a novel about a detective. My life as a writer had to be about the pursuit of the telling detail. If I was going to be successful, I had to find Sergeant Hurt's glasses over and over again in my stories.

At the time, I was just beginning to write fiction. I was working on it at night, not telling anyone. I was experimenting, learning. It would be another five years before I got anything published. But the lesson learned in Sergeant Hurt's office would see me through. Years earlier I had left the detective bureau feeling misunderstood and wronged. I now left feeling like a man with a mission, and a clear path toward completing it.

• • •

THE MOMENTS DIDN'T STOP THEN. They kept coming. I was lucky. I was blessed. I decided to shift my life, to move three thousand miles to the place my literary heroes had written about. On the day I arrived in Los Angeles I sat in a newspaper editor's office being interviewed for a job on the crime beat. He tossed me that day's edition of the paper. The day before, there had been a big crime, a bank heist in which the thieves had gone into the city's labyrinthine storm water tunnel system to get beneath the target bank before tunneling upward. The editor, testing me, asked me how I would do a follow-up on the story. My answer that day passed muster and I was hired. A few years later I would answer with my first published novel, a story that took the bank heist and the tunnels and turned it all into fiction.

Moments. They kept coming. As a reporter in Los Angeles you don't go out to every murder — there are too many and the city's too spread out. You pick and choose. Sometimes it is chosen for you. One morning an editor called me and told me to swing by a murder scene on my way into the office. Just like that, like I was picking up coffee on the way into work. He told me the murder was on Woodrow Wilson Drive in the Hollywood Hills. I went as instructed and got the story. I also got the place where I would put the home of the fictional detective I had secretly begun writing about. A place where he could live and have a view of the city he helped protect, where he could go out on his back deck and take a reading, feel the pulse.

NOTHING WAS LOST. All experiences went into the creative blender and were eventually poured out as something new in my fiction. A story about a man found in the trunk of his Rolls-Royce became a novel about a man found in the trunk of his Rolls-Royce. Stories about cops put on trial became a novel about a cop put on trial.

It wasn't only the cops I drew from. It was the killers, too. The first murder story I ever wrote was for the *Daytona Beach News-Journal.* It was a basic body-found-in-the-woods piece in 1981. But later that body would be connected to one of Florida's most notorious serial killers and I became fascinated by what the cops I knew considered the ultimate kind of evil.

Christopher Wilder was another serial killer. I wrote about him at length and for a time it seemed that he took over my life. As he crossed the country in a desperate effort to elude authorities, I think I took on the same mix of urgency and dread those chasing him felt. It seemed that each day a new woman was abducted or another body was found. It was a big story, perhaps the biggest of my career, but it was an awful story just the same.

Sometimes the killers called me. The phony hit man who was convicted of killing and burying his wife called from jail to say I had been too harsh on him. And then there was Jonathan Lundh, the killer the police feared fit the profile of a serial killer. He was smart, articulate and manipulative. He was also angry at women. The cops went all out to convict him of the one killing they knew about for sure. Lundh used to call me from jail all the time. Not just to protest his innocence, but to manipulate me, to try to find out what the cops were saying to me, what other killings they were telling me about. I remember hanging up the phone each time and feeling lucky that we were separated not only by the phone line but by the concrete and steel of the jail as well. No person I have ever spoken to in my life was creepier than Jonathan Lundh.

It took all of these moments for me to be able to do what I do now. My experiences with cops and killers and days on the crime beat were invaluable to me as a novelist. There could not have been the novelist without there first being the reporter on the crime beat. I could not write about my fictional detective Harry Bosch without having written about the real detectives first. I could not create my killers without having talked to a few of the real ones first.

Not all of the moments saw print in newspapers or in this collection. Not all of them could be written about. I remember one night at a Los Angeles crime scene where I was working backup to another police reporter. It was his story and I was there to help out if it turned into something big. We were standing outside the yellow tape and waiting with many other reporters for the detectives to come out of a house where four people had been found dead. It was all we knew. Four dead. Some were children. We were waiting to see which way the story would go.

I moved down the tape, away from the other reporters. I was hoping to get a private audience because I knew some of the detectives in the house. That's what reporters do. They try to get something for themselves, something nobody else has. You stay on the beat long enough and you get to know the detectives. It gives you an edge.

When the detectives finally came out of the house I waved to the one I knew best. He came over and we spoke privately while the other reporters circled around the other investigators. The man I spoke to was a detective I had spoken to hundreds of times on prior cases. He was a good and tough detective in my estimation. I had never seen him show much emotion, not even when I watched him at cop funerals. There were details of his personality I was already using for my detective Harry Bosch.

"This one's really bad," the detective whispered to me.

He told me the four people dead were a mother and her three young children, all of them shot in the head, all of them in the same bed. He shook his head as if not comprehending the crime. I asked if there was any evidence pointing to who did such a horrible thing.

He nodded.

"Yeah," he said. "She did it. The mother. She killed everybody and left a note."

He then had to walk away from me and I think I saw him wipe a tear out of his eye. And I understood in that moment some of the difficulty, danger and nobility of the job. And I knew I had something more to give Harry Bosch.

PART ONE
THE COPS

THE CALL

LAUDERDALE HOMICIDE

Mayhem and ennui set the tone for a week spent in
the forefront of the battle against a city's murders.

SOUTH FLORIDA SUN-SENTINEL
October 25, 1987

IT HAS BEEN FOUR DAYS since anybody has heard from
or seen Walter Moody and people are thinking that
something is wrong. The tenants at the South Andrews
Avenue apartment building he manages say he hasn't answered his door since Thursday. His parents can't get him

19

on the phone. And he didn't call his boss Saturday when he didn't show up for his part-time truck-driving job.

This is not like Walter, everyone agrees.

It is now 1:40 p.m., Monday, June 29. The happenstance of concern from so many places for Walter Moody results in two Fort Lauderdale police officers and a locksmith coming to his apartment door. There is a small crowd of tenants watching closely.

The three-story apartment building has a Spanish castle motif: white walls, red barrel-tile roof, round turret with small arched windows at the corner. It is a U-shaped building with a neatly kept center courtyard dominated by a shade tree reaching all the way to the roof. There are small bushes and shrubs about the courtyard, all trimmed and cared for by the manager, Walter Moody. The tenants sit on a bench beneath the shade tree and look up to the second-floor walkway where the locksmith has just opened the door to Walter's apartment. The officers go in and find the place ransacked and the door to the master bedroom locked. They call for the locksmith to open it. And after a few moments inside, they call for the homicide squad.

GEORGE HURT has gone home early. His sinuses are acting up and the last few days have been slow. He figures he can take the break. He is sitting on the couch and has the afternoon paper in his hands when he gets The Call.

It's another murder. An apartment manager. No smoking gun. No such luck.

He is told where. He is told when. The how is not yet known. It is Detective Vicki Russo telling him this. She's rolling on it, she says. And so are the others — they being all available members of the homicide squad. George Hurt, sergeant in charge of the squad, says he's rolling too. A routine week in homicide has begun. Hurt hangs up and curses to himself. This is number 38.

Murder in Fort Lauderdale comes in all ways, times, places and circumstances. It is a crime unclassifiable in any way other than by its final result, the taking of life. For George Hurt and the homicide squad the only sure bet is that it comes and comes. This is Monday, June 29, and already there have been 38 homicides this year. There were 42 in all of 1986. The most ever was 52, back in 1981. At this rate, George Hurt is thinking he is going to need another case chart for the wall in the squad room. There could be 60 to 70 murders in Fort Lauderdale this year. That's kind of scary. And that's why he curses each time he gets The Call.

It is hard to account for the numbers. Economics, drugs, heat, full moons, whatever. Hurt's squad has investigated three people shot to death in a fast-food restaurant during a Saturday morning robbery; a high-profile divorce lawyer murdered a few steps from his office elevator; a rock-and-roll singer beaten to death because he was gay. More than a dozen times the victim was either the buyer or seller of drugs when things went wrong. There have been the quiet cases that rated only a few paragraphs in the newspapers, and the big cases that drew the TV trucks with the microwave dishes.

It all adds up to 37 times in six months that the squad has assembled at a scene that defied common sensibilities, the Norman Rockwell portrait of life. And now it is time to gather again. Number 38, Walter Moody, lies cold in bed, his blood four days old on the sheets and pillows, waiting for the homicide squad.

"SMELL THAT?" says George Hurt. "They just rolled the body over in there."

Capt. Al Van Zandt, a supervisor of the detective division, puffs on his cigar so the smell of tobacco will overcome the sickly smell of death.

The two of them are standing outside the door to Walter Moody's apartment. Hurt didn't have to be inside to know what the smell is; he has had years of experience with it. Going back to his stint as head of the department's forensic unit before coming to homicide, and even back 20 years to Vietnam, he says that it seems much of his life has been spent rolling bodies over.

This time he stays mostly outside the apartment with Van Zandt, content to let the forensic investigators and the assistant medical examiner do the work inside.

There are five homicide detectives working the first

hours of the Walter Moody case. One of the first to arrive was Phil Mundy, the squad's senior detective. But after surveying the murder scene and discerning that it was a "whodunit" as opposed to a "smoking gun" case, Mundy returned to the bureau to run record searches on Moody and to coordinate requests that would come from detectives at the scene. His partner, Pete Melwid, is still at the apartment building questioning tenants. So are detectives Mike Walley, Gary Ciani and Vicki Russo. Russo's partner, Kevin Allen, is on the way, called in from a day off. When was Walter last seen? Who were his friends? Who were his enemies? These are the questions the detectives are asking. In the early stages of a case, information is the only available tool.

There is a basic rule to murder investigation; as more time elapses in a case, the chances of solving it grow slimmer. So whenever possible, depending on constrictions of time, the overtime budget, fatigue and so on, Hurt puts all available hands on the initial stages of a case. "It's called trying to figure out what is what and going from there," he says.

The squad has a rotation system for assigning cases to lead detectives. This time partners Russo and Allen are "up." They will be responsible for the case from start to finish. If it is not solved by the group effort in the next few hours, it will be theirs to work alone.

"I haven't had a smoking gun yet this year," Russo says as she starts compiling information in a notebook. "For once, I'd like a gimme — to come in and there would be a victim and over there would be the suspect."

But it hasn't been that way for Russo or the rest of the squad for most of this year.

WHILE THE HOMICIDE detectives corral and question the tenants and the owner of the apartment building, three forensic investigators are inside the apartment looking for fingerprints, photographing and gathering evidence. Dr. Felipe Dominguez, assistant medical examiner, is in the bedroom with the body.

Moody lies faceup on his bed and almost looks as if he is asleep. Almost but not quite. There is a stab wound on his forearm, other cuts, but it is obvious that none were fatal. And there is blood on the sheets and pillow, but the odor of death is not noticeable to anyone without Hurt's nose for it. The killer had left on the air conditioner, slowing decomposition.

The phone in the apartment rings but the detectives don't answer it because there is blood on it and possible fingerprints. After several rings, a tape recording of Walter's voice comes on asking the caller to leave a message. He'll get back to them. The caller is Walter's mother. She is hysterical and wondering what is going on.

"Please, will someone call us as soon as you know what is happening," she pleads after the beep. A detective borrows a phone in another apartment to call.

The detectives interviewing the tenants have come up with three potential avenues of investigation: Walter evicted people from the apartment. Walter was set to be a witness in an upcoming robbery trial. And Walter frequently allowed young men to stay in his apartment in exchange for work around the building.

Working from experience, the detectives pick the third version as the best place to start. And the tenants have provided a description of a young man named Troy who was seen around the apartment as late as Friday afternoon. Let's try to find this Troy, the detectives decide.

Dr. Dominguez is leaving the apartment now and tells Hurt the body is ready to be moved to the medical examiner's office for autopsy. Hurt wants to know the cause of death.

"Knife wound in the back, between the shoulder blades," Dominguez says.

"Big knife? Little knife?"

"Big knife," Dominguez says. "Kitchen knife."

THREE MEN PULL UP to the apartment building in a white van and unload a stretcher. They are the body movers, from a company called Professional. All three are wearing suits and ties, the top buttons on their shirts fastened. They are easily the best-dressed people on the scene. They move in a solemn single file into Walter Moody's apartment to take him on his last trip out.

As they do this, the crime scene begins breaking up. The detectives are heading off in different directions; Melwid to a fast-food restaurant to follow a lead on Troy, Ciani and Walley back to the bureau with three tenants who will help make a composite drawing of the suspect. Van Zandt also heads back. Hurt, Russo and Allen are tying up the last details at the scene before leaving. And inside the apartment, the crime scene technicians are going to take a dinner break. They will have to come back to the apartment later to begin a meticulous and long search into the night for evidence and clues.

When Walter Moody comes out of his apartment for the last time, one tenant is still standing under a shade tree, watching and sipping a beer. Moody is beneath a white sheet. Two of the Professionals — one now has blood on the sleeve and pants of his light blue suit — are straining under the weight of the stretcher, their heels shuffling on the concrete. Once down the stairs, the body is gently placed on a wheeled stretcher and covered with a green velvet blanket. It is then wheeled to the white van. One of the body movers has blue tears tattooed at the corners of his eyes. Somehow it seems appropriate. The people here can't let true sympathy get too much in the way of the work.

At 7 p.m. the yellow plastic barricade tape police had strung across the entrance of the apartment building is taken down. The white van pulls away. The last of the police officers leave the scene. On the walkway outside the murder victim's apartment, the cops have left five empty coffee cups behind. And there are 36 cigarette butts crushed on the cement or dropped in the wood chips spread around the shrubs that Walter Moody had once planted and cared for.

IT IS NEARLY 9 P.M. before the detectives are finished getting a composite of Troy from the witnesses and turning over the collected information to Russo and Allen, the case detectives.

Russo and Allen have several leads. First to check is a name that Mundy came up with on the police computer. It is a person being held in the county jail who gave Walter Moody's address as his own. It might be a former roommate and someone who may know Troy. As Hurt and the other detectives head home for the night, Russo and Allen decide to head to the jail to interview the prisoner. Russo first calls her daughter to say she won't be home until late.

At home, George Hurt watches the first half of a New York Mets and St. Louis Cardinals baseball game on TV before falling asleep. But at 12:30 a.m. he is yanked out of it by the phone. The Call. Fifteen minutes later he is at 600 Southwest 12th Avenue, the corner of Riverside Park, looking at the facedown body of a man with a bullet hole in his back. Number 39.

Walley and Ciani are also there, the partners who are

up on the rotation. Van Zandt is there, cigar in hand, as well as Dominguez and the crime scene detectives. Somebody asks if anybody knows if the Mets won. Somebody else starts an electric generator and a spotlight bathes the body in a harsh white light. Above the grim proceedings the detectives can see storm clouds forming. It will rain soon. They hurry.

The detectives begin talking to witnesses and the two men who had been with the dead man when he was alive just minutes before. They get an idea of what happened.

Michael Connable, 31, was walking with two friends down Sixth Street toward the Riverside Pub. It was midnight dark, and a second group of three men were approaching from the opposite way. As the two groups passed, one of the men from Group Two opened fire. The men of Group One began running. Fifty yards later Connable fell dead a few feet from the door of the Riverside Pub, his blood slowly seeping down an incline on the parking lot toward a storm drain.

Group One did not know Group Two. Group One did not say anything to Group Two. Group One consisted of three gay white men. Group Two consisted of three black men. What did it all mean? What was the motive? Was it random violence? Was it racial? Was it because the men in Group One were gay? In the silence and the darkness, how could the shooter even have known that?

By the time the body movers from Professional arrive — the same three who came for Walter Moody —

the detectives know they have the kind of case that will take a lot of work on the street.

"The only thing we can do is hope to find a snitch," says Walley.

In the last 12 hours, Hurt and his squad have gone zero for two. They've got two whodunits and few clues to the perpetrators. Hurt says he could sure use a smoking gun case. He could also use some sleep.

It starts to rain as Connable is put on the stretcher and carried to the waiting van. The detectives split up and go home. Connable's blood starts to wash down the storm drain. And raindrops fall on the face of the body mover with the tattooed tears.

ON THE WALL in George Hurt's office is a sign that says, "Get off your ass and knock on doors." It might have been made with a salesman in mind, but the slogan is a creed for the homicide detective as well.

Outside his office, the squad room is a quiet place during the days following the Moody and Connable slayings. No murders occur, but the detectives are out on the street, knocking on doors.

Tuesday is autopsy day. But in these cases the autopsies will not provide information critical to solving the cases. So Walley and Ciani and Russo and Allen get the cause of death details on Connable and Moody by phone. There is no need to stand in the tiled room and watch the post-mortem procedures like they do on the TV cop shows.

WHAT IS NEEDED is the almost always boring legwork they don't show on TV. Walley and Ciani spend their time during the rest of the week looking for witnesses in the Connable case, knocking on doors in the Riverside neighborhood, talking to regulars at the Riverside Pub, and checking out the few phone tips that have come in. They are getting nowhere.

The detectives are also working informants, putting the word out into the netherworld network of people who sell street information that this case will bring up to $1,000 for the name of the shooter.

Working informants is one of the ironies of death investigation. Snitches are often criminals themselves; information is gathered on the street by those who work the street — drug dealers and thieves among them. Some wear beepers so they don't miss calls from either customers or the cops. Cops despise them and need them at the same time. But the trouble at the moment is that this time nobody is calling with any information on the Michael Connable case.

"So far, we have nothing," says Walley, a large man who seems more to hunker down over his desk in the squad room than to sit at it.

Russo and Allen are having similar difficulties. Their

efforts to track down the missing Troy are getting them nowhere. The jail prisoner they talked to didn't know any Troy, was no help at all. The fast-food worker named Troy that Melwid came up with can't be located, and might not be the right one anyway. On his application form at the restaurant he put a phony address down. They have tips to three other men who might be their Troy but so far they've hit dead ends.

By Thursday, the only thing for sure about the week's two cases is that both are getting older and harder to solve.

GEORGE HURT is sitting at his desk, shaking his head. He has the reading glasses he usually wears while doing paperwork off and the tip of one of the earpieces clenched in his teeth. The plastic tip is grooved from being clenched there often. It is that kind of job.

Hurt has to shake his head because he is mildly amused, confused and annoyed. In the wake of the week's two slayings he has sat back and watched and read about two occurrences that have left him perplexed. The Connable murder has resulted in a civic meeting between police officials and Riverside residents, and members of the gay community are airing fears that gays in the neighborhood are being targeted by gunmen. So far, the issue has played well in the newspapers and on TV, but the problem is that no one has checked with Hurt or the case detectives, Walley and Ciani, about it. And as far as they are concerned, such fears are unfounded.

"As far as we know at this point, sexual preference had nothing to do with it," Hurt is saying. "We are looking at it as random violence. Some kid with a gun wanted to pop somebody. And he did."

Hurt says the confusion on the case has been further compounded because the night before, one of the local TV news programs out of Miami showed a composite drawing of Troy from the Moody case and said it was the man police were seeking in the Connable shooting. Troy is a white man. The Connable suspect is black.

"Unbelievable, how it gets sometimes," Hurt says.

SHORTLY BEFORE midnight on Thursday, July 2, Johnnie Eddines becomes number 40. Detectives Phil Mundy and Pete Melwid, along with Hurt, are called in from home.

But there is no murder scene to respond to this time. Eddines died in a hospital. He had been found in his car in the 600 block of Northwest 16th Avenue, bleeding from several bullet wounds. He was alive when medical rescuers got there and was transported to Broward General Medical Center. He made it no farther.

The case presents one more irony of homicide investigation. The effort to save Johnnie Eddines had been valiant, but in the end unsuccessful. And, as in most cases where such efforts are made, the crime scene has basically been destroyed, left unpreserved because of rescue efforts inside Eddines' car to save him. It means the effort to save someone may hurt the effort to charge those responsible for his death.

What it also means is that there is no need for the homicide detectives to gather at the scene. Melwid goes by the hospital to gather information on Eddines. Mundy makes a cursory stop at the scene and then goes on to the detective bureau. Hurt heads there as well.

Patrol officers and a midnight shift detective have corralled witnesses to the shooting and are shuttling them to the police station. The victim's car is put on the back of a tow truck and pulled to the police station, too. By midnight, the investigation has begun.

ALL DAYS SHOULD be like Friday. All weeks should end like this.

By 2 a.m., Mundy, Melwid and Hurt are wrapping up the Eddines murder, the first of the week's cases to be closed.

From the witnesses they had learned that they had what was basically a "smoking gun" case; open and shut. Eddines had stolen jewelry from his sister and the man who had given it to her came after him — with two friends and a gun. The detectives spent the morning hours taking statements from the witnesses and preparing warrants for the three suspects. It will just be a matter of catching them. They go home with the case, for the most part, cleared.

The good luck doesn't end with the Eddines case. Vicki Russo comes in to work and gets a little bit of the wish she made outside Walter Moody's apartment four days earlier. The wish for a "gimme."

A friend of the long-sought-after Troy is on the phone saying that Troy wants to come in and talk about Moody. Russo says that's fine, she'll be waiting. A break is a break, even if it comes after a week of chasing dead ends.

When Troy comes in, Russo and Allen sit him down in one of the squad's interview rooms. It is just big enough for a suspect and two interviewers to sit around a table with fluorescent lighting above. The only window, small, square and mirrored, is in the door.

The suspect, whose full name is Troy Tetreault, age 18, begins by saying he was there when Moody was murdered but he didn't do it. He ends by admitting he did it, but only because he was defending himself. Moody was attacking me, he says.

But all of the explanations Troy offers do not explain how someone defending himself would stab his attacker between the shoulder blades and then ransack and rob his home. Troy is charged with first-degree murder, and case number 38 is now counted as cleared.

• • •

WHAT HAS BEEN a bad week has turned out well for the homicide squad. Two out of three cases cleared. Moody's murder is the 31st cleared so far this year, a better than 75 percent rate.

In future weeks, Walley and Ciani would continue to work the Connable slaying but it would remain unsolved. The detectives would get no closer to the three men of Group Two than they were the night one of them opened fire on Group One. In mid-August, Ciani would leave the police department to join a private investigation firm. The file on Connable would remain open on Walley's desk, the detective waiting for a break, a name or a clue that would lead to the shooter. But it wouldn't come, and he would have other cases to follow.

The murder pace would continue in Fort Lauderdale, with the city surpassing the previous year's murder toll of 42 by the end of July and steadily heading toward the all-time high of 53. Two detectives would be temporarily assigned to the squad to help handle the case flow.

Sitting at his desk one day not long after the last week of June, George Hurt would ponder whether the pace was here to stay, whether three murders a week would no longer stand out as an aberration in Fort Lauderdale.

"Believe me, I've been giving it a lot of thought," he says. "But you can't really predict what will happen. I've been hoping that this is just an oddball year. It used to be that four or five homicides a month meant a very heavy month. Now that doesn't look so bad to me."

Whatever happens, Hurt says, the homicide squad is ready.

"Whether there are 45 or 75 homicides, we are here," he says. "I could say that old saying about it being a dirty job but somebody has to do it, but I don't look at it that way. I see it as being a dirty job but somebody has to know how to do it. We know how. We do good work here."

THE OPEN TERRITORY

THE MOB SQUAD

They are the most covert of cops, working in the shadows and watching the underworld. They're closing in on the Open Territory.

SOUTH FLORIDA SUN-SENTINEL
March 29, 1987

L ITTLE NICKY was driving his white Rolls-Royce on Commercial Boulevard in Fort Lauderdale, heading for some dinner, when he saw the blue light in the rearview mirror. He pulled over.

Nicky immediately recognized the cop walking up to his window. It was one of the local detectives who stopped him from time to time to tell him to watch himself down here.

"Mr. Drago, howya doin'?" Nicky said after rolling down the window.

"Fine, Nicky," the detective said. "You got your license with you?"

"I better have that, right Mr. Drago?"

"Yeah, Nicky, you better."

Nicodemo Scarfo, reputed overlord of mob activities in Philadelphia and Atlantic City, and frequent Fort Lauderdale resident, handed Detective Chuck Drago his license. Everything was in order — not like the time Little Nicky's 300-pound driver and bodyguard had handed Drago a counterfeit license and gotten himself arrested.

This time Drago and Scarfo talked almost like old acquaintances. Scarfo said he was leaving town that night, taking a charter up to Pomona Airport near Atlantic City. He'd had enough Florida sun for a while.

"I like your style," Scarfo said. "You're not sneaking around, watching me, trying to sit near me in restaurants, following all the time. You come up to me, man to man. I like that."

Drago smiled. Nicky Scarfo had just paid him the highest possible compliment, without knowing the reason why.

The fact is, Drago and members of the secret police unit he belongs to did sneak around and follow Nicky, go to the track with him and eat at the same restaurants — sometimes at the tables right next to him. They followed his yacht down the Intracoastal, even went to the barbershop with him. They were closer than Scarfo could have guessed, as his compliment to Drago had just confirmed.

THIS IS A TALE from the Open Territory: Broward County, a location unclaimed by any single mob yet a place worked and sometimes called home by members of many of the nation's organized crime families.

It used to be that South Florida was tolerant of the mobsters. But the nature of the territory is changing — and Nicky Scarfo is a sign of the times. After Scarfo had rolled his car window up and gone on his way, Detective Drago went to a phone and made a long-distance call. And that night, when Scarfo stepped off the plane in New Jersey, he was met by FBI agents and the police. He left the airport in handcuffs, facing his second indictment on mob-related charges in as many months.

Drago had done more than just tip his northern counterparts that Little Nicky was on his way. He and his partners' work down here had helped put Scarfo in jail up there. They, too, are a sign of the times, a reason why the Open Territory is changing. They are covert cops, part of a new cult of police intelligence.

• • •

THE SIGN BY THE office's front door changes every so often from one business name to another. But it doesn't really matter what it's called because the name will always be phony and the business will never have any real customers.

The actual name is MIU, short for Metropolitan Organized Crime Intelligence Unit. Plain old MIU goes better with a nondescript operation in a nondescript location.

The detectives assigned to MIU work undercover. They are watchers and gatherers. They move through the streets in cars with windows tinted smoky black, comb through the record stacks at the county courthouse, and access the networks of law enforcement computers.

They watch through telephoto lenses and listen through electronic bugs. They tell their friends never to acknowledge them at the supermarket, the mall, even sitting out by the pool at a waterfront bar. They might be on the job.

MIU's 25 or so detectives come from Broward's major law enforcement agencies. Their business, in simple terms, is raw intelligence. They are experts in the art of surveillance.

For three years they have led a quiet war on organized crime in Broward. Their major weapon is cooperation, the welcome mat they put out for other law enforcement agencies, both near and far.

MIU Detective Steve Raabe likes to tell a story about the time he went down to Miami two years ago to sit in on a hearing held by the Presidential Commission on Organized Crime. The witness that day had once been a major narcotics supplier to New York City. He sat with a black hood over his head and testified about the inner workings of organized crime.

When the witness was finished, one of the commissioners leaned toward his microphone and asked the man what he thought law enforcement was doing wrong. How come organized crime still flourished, despite all the task forces, the commissions, the police agencies, the money spent to combat it?

The witness didn't hesitate. You people have to start communicating, he told the commission. Police have to cooperate with each other. It's the only way.

"Now that sounds kind of strange coming from the mouth of a criminal," says Raabe. "But he hit it right on the head. Crime doesn't stop at the county or city line. There are no boundaries. So the only real hope of law enforcement on any level is cooperation.

"Networking. And that's what MIU is all about."

By quietly documenting the activities of mobsters in Broward County, MIU has become a clearinghouse of intelligence on organized crime activities for federal, state and local authorities. Nicky Scarfo was only one of MIU's targets. Other tales from the Open Territory read like movie scripts.

Even so, MIU remains one of Broward's best-kept secrets. It doesn't seek headlines. "It's not a glamour group going out to make arrests," says Fort Lauderdale Police Chief Ron Cochran, a member of MIU's board of directors. "It has always been behind-the-scenes work. The arrests go to other agencies."

"We're bricklayers," explains Detective Raabe. MIU's operatives help build the cases, put the foundations in place. But they usually aren't around when the building is finished.

It goes back to the days of Capone and Lansky. For half a century, mobsters have come to South Florida to vacation, to retire, or to stay out of reach of the northern police agencies that watched their every move.

"South Florida," says Raabe, "has always been seen by these people as a place where they could be at their leisure, and not worry about being watched by that Philly or New York detective who has been on their back for 20 years."

And Broward County has always been one of the mob's favorite hideaways. By the end of 1985, law enforcement agencies had identified over 600 members and associates of traditional organized crime mobs as residents, full- and part-time, in Broward. They ranged from soldiers to dons. Paul Castellano, head of New York's Gambino organization until his murder in front of a steakhouse in 1985, had a home in Pompano Beach. Gus Alex, an aging, reputed leader of the Chicago mob known as The Outfit, has a Fort Lauderdale address. So did Chicago mob boss Jackie Cerrone until he was imprisoned recently. And so on.

"Organized crime is a growth industry and there is money to be made in Broward County," explains MIU Detective Curt Stuart. "It is safe to say we have seen the interest of all 28 of the nation's organized crime families here."

What that means is that the Open Territory is like few other places where traditional organized crime is found.

"In a city up north, law enforcement has to know the members of maybe one or two crime families," says Sgt. Ken Staab, an MIU supervisor. "Down here we have to know all the families because we've got them all."

And that's why there is an MIU.

Twice in the early 1980s, grand juries evaluating efforts to stop organized crime in Broward concluded that the law enforcement structure seemed ideally suited for the expansion of organized crime.

Investigations were undermanned, efforts fragmented along lines of departmental jurisdictions and jealousies. MIU was established in 1983 after two other task forces had been formed and dismantled because of the same problems.

MIU has a $2 million budget, with each member agency paying the salaries of participants and sharing the overhead. Investigators currently come from police departments in Fort Lauderdale, Pompano Beach, Hollywood and Plantation, along with the Sheriff's Office, the State Attorney's Office and the state Division of Alcoholic Beverages and Tobacco. The head of each agency sits on MIU's board of directors.

"A frequent criticism of law enforcement is that it is too parochial," says Cochran. "While a parochial approach may be adequate in some areas, we feel the best way to go against organized crime is consolidation of expertise. We began with the ambition of creating a first-rate intelligence unit. And I'm satisfied it is one of the best in the country."

MIU directors and detectives often point to the Scarfo case as an example of what the unit can accomplish.

INVESTIGATORS SAY that Nicodemo Scarfo's interest in Broward County coincided with his release from prison in 1984 and rise to the top of the Philadelphia/Atlantic City mob. The diminutive, 57-year-old Scarfo has a criminal record that includes manslaughter and illegal possession of a firearm.

The Philly–South Jersey organization had been run by the "Docile Don," Angelo Bruno, until he was gunned down outside his home in 1980. Nicky took over after Bruno's successor, Phil Testa, was killed by a nail bomb.

Investigators say at least 17 mob-related murders occurred in the City of Brotherly Love during Scarfo's rise to the top of the rackets.

That rise brought Scarfo billing on *Fortune* magazine's list of the most powerful and richest mobsters in the country, his money allegedly coming from unions, numbers, loan-sharking, extortion and gambling.

The indications are that Scarfo was looking to move up the *Fortune* list. He started routinely making lengthy visits to Fort Lauderdale. In 1985, he set up his southern operations on Northeast 47th Street near the Intracoastal Waterway, in a two-story, Spanish-style house with an iron gate out front. He put up a sign on the front wall that named the place Casablanca South. The yacht docked out back was also called Casablanca, but there was a smaller postscript painted below the name. Usual Suspects, it said, a wry reference to the police inspector's instruction in the famed Bogart movie: "Round up all the usual suspects."

It's a funny thing about the house and boat, Detective Drago says: Scarfo didn't own them. Investigators are still trying to learn how he came to control them.

"Nicky liked the house and the boat," Drago says. "So he took them. When Little Nicky wants something, he just takes it. You don't argue."

By all estimates of law enforcement authorities, Scarfo wanted to take Broward County, or at least part of it.

Florida had an upcoming referendum on casino gambling, and investigators believe that Scarfo was preparing to direct organized crime's interests if casinos came to pass.

A decade earlier, Scarfo had done the same thing in Atlantic City. The President's Commission on Organized Crime named him as the chief figure behind the mob's influence in the casino construction industry there. Coincidentally, MIU investigators say, contractors who bid against the mob companies had a tendency to get killed.

Shortly after Scarfo arrived in Fort Lauderdale, the FBI initiated what was called the Southern Summit, a law enforcement conference on organized crime influences in the South. They named Nicodemo Scarfo as their primary target and directed MIU, a relatively unknown agency less than two years old, to work in concert with investigators building cases in New Jersey and Philadelphia against the reputed mob lord.

MIU would turn out to be a major conduit of raw intelligence on Scarfo, the reason being that Scarfo believed he had a free rein in the Open Territory.

"He was a priority up here, but I'm sure he thought he wouldn't be much of a priority down there," says Sgt. Bill Coblantz of the New Jersey State Police mob intelligence unit. "They've got a lot of other organized people to watch down there. So he went to South Florida without the same kind of police paranoia he had up here. He relaxed. That's what Fort Lauderdale is for, right?"

But Nicky was wrong.

The mansion he had chosen for his Casablanca South was on a remote, dead-end street, but it faced an empty lot that bordered a canal. And across that canal was a five-story condominium complex.

While Nicky and his associates met at Casablanca South, their cars lined up and down the street, Chuck Drago and other detectives from MIU, the FBI, even Philadelphia and New Jersey, would be watching from behind the darkened windows of one of the upstairs condos across the canal. The view was good and the FBI kept the lease on the place for a year. The cameras were always rolling.

The detectives looked out on a world not previously documented in the Open Territory. While law enforcement pressure in northern cities had made the big meetings of crime families largely things of the past, Scarfo was in Fort Lauderdale hosting meetings so large that he needed a caterer. Sometimes, he'd take 15 or 20 people, documented by police as crime associates, out for rides on his yacht.

"It was amazing what we were seeing," recalls Staab, the MIU supervisor. "These other agents would come here from up north and they couldn't believe how open this guy was being."

"When you see them go into a restaurant and the chefs and the waitresses all walk out and stand around while the doors are locked for the meeting inside, you really get an idea of what is going on down here," says Raabe.

Little Nicky's associations were not only with members of his own crew. The covert cops watched him meet in Fort Lauderdale with high-ranking representatives from many of the country's major mobs — Colombo, Lucchese, Buffalino and so on.

"The nature of intelligence work is to take raw information and hypothesize, come up with theories of what is happening," says Raabe. "So we see Nicky meeting all these people. Business is obviously being discussed. We can't say for sure what was happening, but we have a good idea."

And these meetings came with all the clichés of movies like *The Godfather.* There was the reverential treatment of Mafia leaders, the ceremonial kissing of cheeks and hands.

"Sometimes it got to be funny," Drago says. "We'd see the cars pull up with 10 or 15 guys getting out for a meeting and they'd be circling all over the front yard trying to make sure they kissed or hugged everybody."

JUST LIKE THE MOBSTERS, police don't like offending their own. Law enforcement agencies are territorial, careful not to encroach on others' turf without invitation.

It is the axiom of parochialism that Chief Cochran of Fort Lauderdale speaks of.

And that axiom flies in the face of MIU's all-for-one, one-for-all concept of sharing intelligence among law enforcement agencies. After years of working cases, MIU has neither been joined by all the police agencies in Broward County nor has it replaced the organized crime or intelligence units of its member agencies. Instead, it continues to work with them and, as always, remains quietly in the background.

"It would be my hope that MIU would one day be the organized crime investigative enterprise in this county," says Cochran. But in the meantime, investigators in Pennsylvania and New Jersey, and maybe even people like Nicky Scarfo, probably have a better understanding of what MIU is all about than the Broward citizens who help pay for it.

"MIU is becoming a highly respected information bank on what these types of OC characters are doing down there," says Coblantz of the New Jersey police. "Put it this way — on the Scarfo case, MIU has given us leads that we are still tracking down."

WHILE NICKY SCARFO was under the eye of MIU in Fort Lauderdale, two high-ranking members of his organization were in Philadelphia talking to the FBI and then to a grand jury. There were also 800 tapes of wiretaps. And from Fort Lauderdale came the MIU dossiers and indications that Scarfo was running the organization from Casablanca South. On Nov. 3, 1986, he was arrested while on a trip to New Jersey. A grand jury had indicted him and 17 associates for conspiracy and racketeering.

A day later in Florida, the casino issue was defeated at the polls.

Scarfo was released on bail and returned to Fort Lauderdale once more, but the grand jury wasn't through. While he lay on the chaise longue behind Casablanca South, Scarfo's empire was being quietly dismantled. He would face still another indictment.

On Jan. 7 of this year, Little Nicky's white Rolls pulled into Fort Lauderdale–Hollywood International Airport and the gray-haired, well-tanned man was dropped off at a charter airline's front gate. Scarfo was traveling light — no bodyguard.

He went into the airport lounge for a drink before boarding. He didn't know it then, but a couple of hours later he would land in New Jersey and the FBI and police would be waiting. Detective Drago had tipped them earlier that day after stopping Scarfo on his way to dinner. This would be the night that Scarfo would be jailed without bond for his second indictment.

Over at the bar, two men sat and watched Scarfo until he walked to the boarding gate. They followed and watched while he went down the loading ramp.

Maybe Nicky had a premonition. Maybe the back of his neck was burning. Whatever it was, something made him turn and look back as he got to the plane's door. He saw a man standing at the other end of the ramp looking at him. It was a man Nicky had never seen before. Steve Raabe, detective from MIU, stepped out of character for that moment and smiled. Then he waved good-bye to Nicky Scarfo. A send-off from the Open Territory.

CROSSING THE LINE

LAPD FOREIGN
PROSECUTION UNIT

South of the border is no longer safe for criminals.

LOS ANGELES TIMES
December 13, 1987

SEVEN YEARS AGO, the body of first-grader Lisa Ann Rosales was found dumped in a ditch near her home in Pacoima. She had been sexually molested and strangled.

The case was not an easy one for the Los Angeles Police Department — it took a tip five years later for detectives to identify a suspect, and then they discovered that the man had fled to his native Mexico.

In previous years, the case might have ended there, with police thwarted because the suspect was beyond the reach of U.S. laws. The problem, which had long frustrated American law enforcement officials, was that Mexico refuses to extradite its own citizens to the United States for trial, despite the existence of an extradition treaty between the two countries.

But this time the case did not end. Detectives turned to a new squad in the LAPD, the foreign prosecution unit.

Six months after the Los Angeles detectives decided that they knew who killed Lisa Ann Rosales, Mexican authorities were handed a complete file on Luis Raul Castro, translated into Spanish, and were even told where he could be found. They took the case from there.

Today, Castro stands convicted in a Mexican federal court of murder. He is expected to be sentenced by the end of the year and could serve up to 40 years in a Mexican jail.

"Before we had the foreign prosecution unit, people were literally getting away with murder," said Lt. Keith Ross, supervisor of the unit. "The fact was we were not actively pursuing Mexican suspects that fled to Mexico. That has changed."

The Rosales case is one of many examples of how Los Angeles crime means Mexican prison time since the four-member unit began working with Mexican authorities in 1985. Since then, 48 Los Angeles cases — all but three involving murder — have been brought in Mexico. More than half the suspects have been captured, convicted and jailed there.

'Is It Legal?'

Scattered cases have been brought in other countries as well, including one in France.

"The first thing people ask is 'Can you do that? Is that legal?'" Ross said. "The answer is that it is a legitimate means of prosecution that is available to us."

But some legal observers question whether suspects should face Mexican justice for American crimes. They argue that Mexico's justice system affords defendants few of the protections of the U.S. system — most notably, defendants do not have a chance to face their accusers; the testimony of the American witnesses is delivered solely through documents.

"My first reaction is that it presents an enormous problem," said Leon Goldin, executive director of the Los Angeles chapter of the National Lawyers Guild. "We are talking about the LAPD, acting as an arm of our government, using court procedures in Mexico that wouldn't pass muster here in a moment."

No Acquittals

The record shows that the California law enforcement officials are almost certain to go home happy after bringing a case to Mexico. No case brought by the LAPD has yet to result in an acquittal.

It is a great contrast to the situation Los Angeles police faced when they conducted a 1984 study that prompted creation of the foreign prosecution unit.

In that study, according to Ross, police reviewed all outstanding murder warrants — cases in which a suspect had been identified, but no one arrested. Of 267 people being sought, about 200 had Latino surnames, he said.

"That gave us the strong feeling that a large number of suspects were fleeing to Mexico and finding sanctuary," he said. "There was no department-wide procedure for tracking, arresting and prosecuting them."

"There was a lot of frustration," said Detective Arturo Zorrilla, noting that the attitude of most officers was, "Let's file the case away and hope [the suspect] comes back across."

Extradition Treaty

In theory, prosecutors here could have sought extradition on any of the suspects confirmed as being in Mexico. The two countries have an extradition treaty that provides for Mexican citizens to be returned to the United States to face trial for serious crimes. But, a U.S. Justice Department spokesman said, "It has not occurred, ever."

The refusal to extradite, officials said, is rooted in a

firm belief in Mexican law that Mexican citizens who commit crimes outside the country should be prosecuted by Mexican authorities.

U.S. law, on the other hand, provides that U.S. citizens who commit crimes in other countries should be subject to prosecution there. (About half a dozen American citizens have been extradited to Mexico in the last decade to face trial, according to the Justice Department.)

On Books since 1928

The different approaches are reflected in a provision of Mexico's penal code that allows for the prosecution of foreign crimes. Although on the books since 1928, the provision was infrequently used until recently because other countries' law enforcement agencies rarely brought cases to the attention of Mexican authorities.

Before the Los Angeles foreign prosecution unit was formed in April 1985, the LAPD, like most U.S. police agencies, did not have formal procedures for cutting through the diplomatic red tape to pursue cases in Mexico. Few detectives even knew it was possible.

Today, a U.S. Justice Department international law specialist said, the Los Angeles unit is in "the forefront of using this tactic."

Operating under the fugitive division headed by Ross, the foreign prosecution unit is led by two homicide squad veterans, Detectives Zorrilla and Gilberto Moya.

Both see their jobs as equal parts detective work and diplomacy.

The Murder Book

To file cases in Mexico, the unit, whose members are bilingual, compiles a written record of the case in Spanish. Affidavits, witness statements, photographs and descriptions of evidence are put into a report they call the "murder book."

This consolidation and translation is often the longest part of the procedure, usually lasting several weeks. The Lisa Ann Rosales case filled four thick files.

The district attorney's office must then formally relinquish jurisdiction of a case, an action that is not taken lightly. Prosecutors acknowledge that because of the U.S. Constitution's protection against double jeopardy, if they seek trial of a case in Mexico and do not get a guilty verdict, any attempt to refile the charges in the United States would be quickly challenged.

Norman Shapiro, a deputy district attorney who handles the foreign cases, said the decision depends mainly on the prospects for prosecution in the United States and a certainty that the suspect will not return from Mexico.

'We Have Been Satisfied'

"We have to have solid information that the suspect is down there," Shapiro said. "When we have that, we have been quite willing to let Mexico prosecute. We have been satisfied with the results."

Of the 26 Los Angeles cases that have made it through the Mexican justice system, according to the foreign prosecution unit, all have resulted in convictions. And although Mexico does not have the death penalty, officers familiar with U.S. cases tried there said prison sentences seem to be slightly longer. Because of differences in laws, making exact comparisons is impossible.

Before the case travels to Mexico, the Mexican Consulate in Los Angeles must certify the authenticity of the investigative documents. In practice, this usually means confirming that a crime was committed and that the investigating officers are legitimate.

Then, once officers have determined through informants and other detective work where a suspect is in Mexico, the unit moves.

Checked Weapons at Border

This year, the detectives have checked their weapons at the border and crossed into Mexico an average of twice a month.

Occasionally they travel with Mexican police to observe the arrests, but most often they wait at police stations or hotels until a suspect is in custody or local police determine that he or she cannot be found. Moya said the officers go to Mexico to streamline the filing process, strengthen relations with authorities there and be available to offer additional case details or even question suspects themselves.

The officers make no secret of the value of the social side of the visits.

"Diplomacy and image are important," Moya said. "You make concessions, courtesies to their protocol. You pay your respects. We don't want to meddle in the internal workings of the law enforcement of another country. We work within their customs."

Protocol Observed

On a recent trip to Mexicali to present evidence in connection with an East Los Angeles murder, Moya and José Herrera, the case detective, did not go directly to the prosecutor who would handle the case.

They first went to see the director of the state police, whose men had caught the suspect a week earlier based on leads Moya and Herrera had provided. Then there were several meetings with Mexican detectives and police administrators to shake hands and pay respects.

The Los Angeles officers offered the Mexicans small gifts of basic equipment not provided by their own department: flashlights, handcuffs, notepads, even bullets. The Californians had purchased the items in the United States with their own money.

When the detectives finally got to the office of Angel Saad, attorney general of the state of Baja, their stay in Mexico was nearly over. Saad looked over the file, grimaced at photographs of the victim's body and asked detailed questions about the legal and diplomatic procedures they had followed.

After a 45-minute meeting, Saad finally placed the "murder book" in the hands of one of his prosecutors.

Notified of Outcome

In a year or so, after the process of trial and appeal is completed, Mexican authorities will officially notify Los Angeles police of the outcome.

American law enforcement officials acknowledge that procedural differences make it easier to get convictions in Mexico than in the United States.

Once a case is accepted for prosecution in Mexico, a defendant is assumed to be guilty and then has to prove his innocence. There is no bail allowed in murder cases, no jury trials and guidelines on the admissibility of evidence are less stringent.

LAPD foreign prosecution unit officers said they know of no instance in which a witness in a Los Angeles murder case, detectives included, went to Mexico to testify. Instead, Mexican prosecutors rely upon the witness accounts and affidavits supplied by police.

Attorneys Disturbed

That the defendants thus are denied the opportunity to face their accusers, a cornerstone of the U.S. justice system, is disturbing to some attorneys.

"No one says a criminal should go unpunished," said Jaime Cervantes, a former president of the Mexican-American Bar Assn. in Los Angeles. "But this country has a long-developed concept of how someone is proven guilty of a crime and there is something fundamentally unfair about going to another country to convict and punish them."

Peter Shey, chairman of the international law committee of the local National Lawyers Guild, also questioned the Mexican prosecutions.

"Basic notions of fundamental fairness are either non-existent or rarely employed in their justice system," Shey said. "If people are required to stand trial in Mexico for crimes in the United States, they would be placed at a significant disadvantage."

'A Jaundiced Eye'

Lt. Ross, the unit's supervisor, said he believes that such concerns are unfounded.

"I think a lot of people have tended to view Mexican justice with a jaundiced eye," he said. "But that is an American perception and it is a misconception. Mexico has a very legitimate legal system that operates very well."

Ross and his fellow officers contend that a murder suspect who flees to avoid prosecution in Los Angeles is accepting the justice system of the country he runs to.

"You have to accept the risks that you have incurred by fleeing," Moya said.

Much like the LAPD unit, the California attorney general's office has developed specialists in bringing cases to Mexico. The state's chief expert is Ruben R. Landa, a special agent with the attorney general's office in San Diego, who took his department's first murder case to Mexico in 1980.

70 Murder Cases Brought

Since then, Landa has helped various California police departments bring 70 murder cases to Mexico, 14 so far in 1987, more than in any previous year. About 20 of the cases have worked their way through Mexican courts, he said, all resulting in convictions, although one of those was thrown out on appeal.

"Now it's sort of snowballing," he said. "More and more detectives are finding out that this is a way to go with their cases."

One benefit for U.S. authorities is financial. Mexico pays for prosecuting the cases, and police officials estimate that it costs American taxpayers less than $1,000 in travel and other expenses to bring a case there, an amount that pales in comparison to the costs of jailing, prosecuting and defending a murder suspect in Los Angeles.

"You are probably talking about saving thousands of dollars on every case," Ross said.

'Two-Way Street'

But Angel Saad, the Baja attorney general, said the arrangement does not just help the U.S. agencies.

"It is a two-way street with positive results for both countries," he said. "For Mexico, it signifies its willingness to punish its citizens that commit crimes in foreign countries."

A more tangible way the relationship pays off for Mexico, police say, is when the foreign prosecution unit, acting on tips from Mexican police, locates Mexicans in Los Angeles who are suspected of crimes in their own country. So far this year, 13 such suspects have been arrested by immigration authorities in Los Angeles as illegal aliens and returned to Mexico with the help of the unit. Because they are illegal aliens, they can be shipped back without lengthy extradition proceedings.

Other Kinds of Cases

Although most of its time has been spent on murder cases in Mexico, the foreign prosecution unit has been used on occasion in child abuse, robbery and auto theft investigations. And its officers have pursued murder cases in other countries where laws allow prosecution of foreign crimes. Two cases have been brought in El Salvador, one in France and one investigation is pending in Honduras.

The crimes that lead the officers across the border are quite varied, involving both Mexican and American victims.

Lorraine Kiefer, 70, was a well-liked Van Nuys widow and retired real-estate broker who worked without pay at an American Cancer Society thrift shop. In 1980, she had married Gilberto Flores, a longtime acquaintance who was 38 years her junior. Four years later, police said, Flores hired a second man, Andreas Hernandez Santiago, to kill her for $5,000.

Filed in Mexico

After detectives unraveled the Oct. 2, 1984, killing, the case was filed in Mexico, where the two men, both Mexican nationals, had fled. Santiago was arrested in Oaxaca and later convicted and sentenced to 18 years in prison. Flores is still being sought.

In one of the first cases handled by the unit in 1985, Juan Francisco Rocha, 36, was arrested in Monterrey, Mexico, for the killing in Hollywood of his girlfriend, Brenda Joyce Abbud, a decade earlier. She had been doused with paint thinner and set on fire.

"Many of the cases have strong impacts on their communities," Zorrilla said.

The Dec. 8, 1980, killing of Lisa Ann Rosales was such a case, prompting the Los Angeles City Council to offer a $25,000 reward for information leading to an arrest. A local high school started a college scholarship in Lisa's name and an elementary school named a garden after her.

There were few solid leads until a woman called police anonymously in 1985, saying her conscience bothered her and that she wanted them to know that Castro, who worked as a maintenance man at the Rosales home, was the killer. That lead gave the case a new focus, and police said more evidence was uncovered against Castro.

Castro, who had returned to Mexico weeks after the killing, confessed shortly after he was arrested in Mexicali in 1986, according to police in both countries.

COPS ACCUSED

MURDER SUSPECT SEEKS TO CLEAR NAME WITH LAWSUITS

Mary Kellel-Sophiea says homicide investigators wrongfully tried to pin her husband's slaying on her. The detectives still believe she's guilty.

LOS ANGELES TIMES
September 15, 1991

MARY KELLEL-SOPHIEA says she is on trial for murder. But it was her choice.

For more than two months last year, she faced a possible death sentence after being charged with the murder of her estranged husband. On Jan. 31, 1990, Gregory

Sophiea was stabbed to death in his bed in the Shadow Hills home that the couple had shared for five years.

But then a prosecutor dropped the charges against her, telling a judge he did not have enough evidence to proceed with the case in court.

A year and a half later, the additional evidence has not been found. But Kellel-Sophiea is back in court. She is suing her accusers, charging two Los Angeles police detectives with violating her rights by arresting her without cause and conspiring to frame her with a murder she did not commit.

The two-week-old civil trial before a jury in U.S. District Court has unfolded much like that of a murder trial.

Detectives testified about their investigation and identified an 18-year-old transient who has been convicted of the murder and who they believe conspired with Kellel-Sophiea to kill her husband. A medical examiner discussed the details of the autopsy. A next-door neighbor told the jury about finding the dead man and the blood-spattered butcher knife.

Though no death sentence rides on the jury's verdict, the 10-member panel will, in effect, be asked to cast judgment on Kellel-Sophiea, deciding whether she has been wrongfully pursued by two obsessed investigators or possibly is a killer who has not only gotten away with her crime but is now seeking monetary damages from her pursuers.

Kellel-Sophiea, 40, now lives in Long Beach. She is seeking unspecified damages from Detectives Woodrow Parks and Gary Milligan. She believes the jury will exonerate her by finding that the detectives wrongfully arrested her. She said such a verdict will finally help end the suspicion that surrounds her.

"If I was guilty, why wouldn't I just go on with my life and thank God I had gotten away with it?" she asked in an interview last week. "Why would I go through with this trial? It's like a murder trial. If I was guilty, I wouldn't be sitting here."

The lawsuit focuses on what happened in the early morning hours of Jan. 31 at the Sophiea family's Orcas Avenue house and whether detectives assigned to the case correctly and honestly interpreted the evidence left by a killer. Kellel-Sophiea claims they did not.

"They threw this woman on a freight train to hell, and they still are trying to shovel coal on the fire," said Ken Clark, one of her attorneys.

According to testimony at the trial, Gregory Sophiea and his wife argued on the last night of his life.

The couple had separated after 10 years of marriage but had agreed to meet at the house they owned — and where Gregory, a salesman and caterer, was staying — to discuss its sale.

Death Followed Quarrel

Kellel-Sophiea, a former advertising executive, testified that the couple argued over furniture she needed for her new apartment in Long Beach, and related financial matters.

Later, Gregory went to sleep in the master bedroom while his wife slept in another bedroom and their 6-year-old daughter, Kristen, slept in a third room.

In a tape-recorded interview with police on the day of the murder, Kellel-Sophiea said she was awakened shortly after 3 a.m. by a noise and heard a gurgling sound. Knowing her husband was asthmatic, she rushed to his bedroom and saw him lying on his back on the water bed gasping for breath.

She said she saw blood on the sheets and assumed he had injured himself — something that had occurred once before during a morning asthma attack. She did not notice the stab wounds on her husband's chest and neck, she told the detectives.

Though there was a phone on the nightstand Kellel-Sophiea ran to another phone in the house, dialed 911 to report her husband could not breathe and then ran to a next-door neighbor's house for help. While the neighbor, Larry Rotoli, went into the bedroom to try to aid Sophiea, Kellel-Sophiea remained at the front of the house to direct paramedics inside.

When the paramedics arrived moments later, they found Gregory Sophiea dead, with seven stab wounds in the upper body.

Kellel-Sophiea was taken to the Foothill Division police station to await questioning while several detectives gathered at the scene of the crime. Among them were Parks, who had eight years' experience as a homicide detective, and Milligan, who was working his first case as homicide detective trainee. They would be the lead detectives assigned to the case.

Among the pieces of evidence awaiting the detectives was a bloody butcher knife on the bedroom floor. They found the window in one of the bathrooms open to the backyard and an undamaged screen leaning on an outside wall. There was dirt on the toilet seat and the bathroom floor.

Bloodstains were found in other parts of the house, and there were bloody fingerprints on a backyard fence. They also found pry marks on the outside of a rear door.

On the surface, evidence seemed to indicate that someone had broken into the house through the bathroom window, and escaped through the window and over the fence after stabbing Sophiea. But the detectives, after conducting a routine preliminary investigation, came to a different conclusion.

No Footprints

Parks and Milligan testified that they found no foot-prints in the dirt below the bathroom window. The de-tectives determined the window screen could not have been removed from the outside without being damaged. And using an oblique lighting technique, they deter-mined that dust on the stone pathway that led to the bathroom window had not been disturbed — indicating no one had walked there that morning.

They also found chemical traces of what could have been blood in two sinks and a bathtub in the house.

The detectives developed the theory that the break-in had been staged to throw the investigation off course.

"We were all in unanimous agreement that this was not a burglary," Milligan testified last week. "I don't be-lieve anyone went in or out of that window."

Burglary eliminated, their suspicions turned to the widow. The detectives testified it was their opinion that the victim had been dead at least an hour before Kellel-Sophiea said she saw him struggling for breath and dialed 911. Also, a chemical test of her hands re-vealed traces of blood, though she had said she did not remember touching her husband before seeking help. Most of all, it was her story that did not ring true, the de-tectives said.

"This man with seven holes in his body was having an

asthma attack?" Milligan testified. "What she told us was incredible. I wondered . . . why anyone would look at this individual and say he had an asthma attack."

The two detectives questioned Kellel-Sophiea at the Foothill station for two hours, but she did not change her original story, according to a transcript of the interview, which was played for jurors. Instead, she became hysterical when told her husband had died of stab wounds, not an asthma attack, and that she was under arrest:

Parks: "You murdered the guy."

Kellel-Sophiea: "Oh, come on. I don't understand any of this. . . . What do you mean? I don't even know what you are talking about. . . ."

Parks: "Well, let me tell you real quick. . . . I'm talking about you going to jail . . . killing your husband."

Kellel-Sophiea: "I never . . . I'm no killer. I don't have that in me. . . . I don't believe this."

Parks: "Well, believe it."

Kellel-Sophiea: ". . . I didn't do anything wrong. Why would I? This has got to be a dream."

Kellel-Sophiea was jailed and was arraigned two days later on murder charges in San Fernando Municipal Court. She pleaded not guilty.

Investigation of the case continued, and in mid-February, the investigators learned that the bloody fingerprints on the fence did not belong to Kellel-Sophiea as they had expected. Instead, they belonged to an

18-year-old drug abuser and former psychiatric patient named Tony Moore.

On Feb. 20, 1990, the detectives arrested Moore, and during a six-hour interrogation, Moore gave a variety of versions of what happened Jan. 31, alternately implicating himself and Kellel-Sophiea as the killer.

David Romley, another of Kellel-Sophiea's attorneys, said a tape recording of the Moore interrogation is a key part of his client's case against the detectives. He said the tape shows the detectives fell into "tunnel investigation" and "suspect of convenience" syndromes by steering Moore toward their set belief that the burglary was staged and that Kellel-Sophiea was involved.

"They just tried to mold everything into their conclusion," Romley said.

According to a transcript of the taped interrogation, Moore initially denied ever being in the Sophiea house, but when told that his bloody fingerprints were found at the scene, he replied, "OK, you got me."

Moore then told the two detectives step by step how he had broken into the house through a bathroom window and took a butcher knife from the kitchen. He said he stabbed Sophiea when the man awoke while Moore was in his bedroom looking for items to steal.

But the detectives told Moore he was lying, and he changed his story to include Kellel-Sophiea as the killer. He said she paid him $600 to kill her husband, but he said she did it herself when he was unable to go through with it.

Moore said he and Kellel-Sophiea then staged the break-in to make it appear that a burglar had killed Sophiea.

Changing Stories

Moore changed his story two more times as the interrogation continued, going back to admitting that he had killed Sophiea while burglarizing the house, then once again saying Kellel-Sophiea was the killer, this time adding that he was romantically involved with her.

Kellel-Sophiea branded as preposterous Moore's accusations that she was involved with him or the killing. Romley said the detectives led Moore "down the garden path" by feeding him information about Kellel-Sophiea and the evidence during the early stage of the interrogation, which allowed him to later concoct her involvement in the killing.

Romley said he intends to play the tape for the jury this week, though Assistant City Atty. Honey A. Lewis, who is defending the two detectives, has opposed allowing jurors to hear it. Lewis, Parks and Milligan declined to discuss the case before completion of the trial.

Following Moore's arrest, Kellel-Sophiea was rearraigned on murder charges, this time including an allegation of murder for financial gain, which carries a possible death penalty. The financial gain allegation was added because police and prosecutors believed Kellel-Sophiea was motivated to kill her husband to collect insurance money and to avoid having to share the proceeds from the sale of the house.

Moore later pleaded guilty to murder and was sentenced to 27 years to life in prison. But detectives were unable to find evidence substantiating Moore's claims about Kellel-Sophiea's involvement, and charges against her were dropped on April 5, 1990, the day a preliminary hearing was set to begin.

Deputy Dist. Atty. Craig R. Richman testified during the federal trial last week that the charges could be reinstated if additional evidence against Kellel-Sophiea is ever found. He also said he has seen no evidence that dissuades him from his belief that the burglary at the Sophiea house was staged.

Parks and Milligan also are unswayed in their suspicions of the widow. Both have testified that they still believe she was involved in her husband's slaying.

"I think she and Tony Moore entered into a conspiracy," Milligan said.

Kellel-Sophiea's attorneys have sought to bolster her innocence with a variety of testimony and witnesses.

Though the detectives said Sophiea was dead an hour before his wife sought help, Deputy Medical Examiner Dr. Irwin Goldin, who conducted the Sophiea autopsy, testified that it was impossible to pinpoint the time of death within the two hours before paramedics arrived. Two private experts in criminology have testified that the bathroom screen can easily be removed from outside the house, contrary to the detectives' view.

Wounds Unnoticed

Rotoli, the neighbor whom Kellel-Sophiea went to for help that night, testified that, although he spent two minutes attempting to render help to Sophiea, he also did not notice any stab wounds on the man's body — largely because the victim's chest was thickly covered with hair.

Rotoli also said he washed blood off his hands in the kitchen sink. And a forensic expert testified that tests for trace amounts of blood found in the other sink and bathtub and on Kellel-Sophiea's hands could be inaccurate or could be identifying blood unrelated to the slaying.

Kellel-Sophiea's attorneys charge that all of their information was available to the detectives immediately after the slaying but that they bungled the case by focusing too soon on Kellel-Sophiea. And now, having accused her, they refuse to back down.

"Before they even got out to the crime scene they were thinking the wife did it," Romley said. "Then they saw the burglary evidence, and they didn't want to look at it. They had a predetermined mind-set. They already had her convicted."

Kellel-Sophiea said she remains fearful that she could lose her freedom again.

"I don't know if they will ever stop," she said of Parks and Milligan. "That's why I am doing this. I want to stop them from doing this to anyone else."

WIFE STILL A SUSPECT
IN HUSBAND'S DEATH
AFTER LOSING SUIT
September 26, 1991

A police investigation of Mary Kellel-Sophiea as a suspect in the stabbing death of her husband continued Wednesday, a day after two detectives were cleared of wrongdoing in her lawsuit charging they had falsely arrested and conspired to frame her.

A federal court jury deliberated only 35 minutes before returning a verdict in favor of Los Angeles Detectives Woodrow Parks and Gary Milligan.

Kellel-Sophiea, 40, had sued the officers, saying they had bungled the investigation of the Jan. 31, 1990, stabbing of Gregory Sophiea in the couple's Shadow Hills home. The lawsuit contended that the detectives wrongly focused on her as a suspect when it was clear that a burglar had killed her husband.

Kellel-Sophiea was arrested the morning of the killing, but murder charges were dropped two months later when prosecutors said they did not have enough evidence. An 18-year-old transient, who police contend conspired with her to kill her husband, later pleaded guilty and was sentenced to 27 years in prison.

Parks, who continues to handle the investigation, said Kellel-Sophiea remains a suspect. He said studies of scientific evidence, including DNA analysis, are ongoing. He declined to discuss that evidence.

"This isn't a holy mission, but it is an open case," Parks said. "I don't have any personal vendetta. She ought to be brought to justice because there are a lot of things here that show she did have something to do with her husband's killing."

Milligan, who now works as a narcotics investigator, could not be reached for comment.

During the three-week trial in U.S. District Court, attorneys for Kellel-Sophiea sought to show that she was innocent and that the man later convicted of the slaying had acted alone.

At the time of the killing, Kellel-Sophiea and her husband were separating and slept in different bedrooms in their Orcas Street house. She testified that at 3 a.m. on Jan. 31, 1990, she heard and saw her husband struggling for breath, and thinking that he was having an asthma attack dialed 911 and ran to a neighbor's house for help. Rescuers found that Sophiea had been stabbed to death, and police discovered that a bathroom window was open and the screen removed.

Parks and Milligan testified that the evidence indicated that the burglary had been "staged" to throw off the investigation. They said contradictions in Kellel-Sophiea's statements along with other evidence — including blood found on the floor of her bedroom — focused their attention on her as a suspect.

Two weeks after Kellel-Sophiea was arrested, the detectives traced bloody fingerprints found on a fence at the house to Tony Moore, an 18-year-old Sun Valley transient. Moore was arrested, and during nine hours of interrogation he gave several versions of what happened, implicating himself and at times saying Kellel-Sophiea took part in the killing.

Though Moore's statements about Kellel-Sophiea were never corroborated, the investigators continue to believe that the burglary was staged and that she was involved.

Before jury deliberations began, Judge James M. Ideman dismissed the lawsuit's allegation that the investigators were conspiring to frame Kellel-Sophiea, ruling that there was no evidence of such behavior.

Deputy City Atty. Honey A. Lewis, who defended the detectives, said the jurors were left to decide whether the investigators acted in good faith when they arrested Kellel-Sophiea. Whether she was guilty or innocent in the slaying was not at issue, Lewis said.

"That's an unsolved mystery," she said. "That wasn't under consideration. The issue was whether the detectives had probable or reasonable cause to arrest her. The jury determined there was good reason for the detectives to make the arrest."

One of Kellel-Sophiea's attorneys, Ken Clark, said her case was hurt when Ideman ruled that jurors could not hear a tape recording of the Moore interrogation that he said showed the detectives manipulated the suspect into implicating her in the slaying.

Clark said the verdict will probably be appealed.

DEATH SQUAD

POLICE SURVEILLANCE UNIT
KILLS 3 ROBBERY SUSPECTS

LOS ANGELES TIMES
February 13, 1990

T HREE SUSPECTED ROBBERS were killed and a fourth was wounded early Monday by nine officers from a controversial Los Angeles police squad who watched the suspects force their way into a closed McDonald's restaurant in Sunland and rob its manager at gunpoint.

Shortly after the suspected robbers climbed into their

getaway car — and one pointed a gun at the officers, police said — the officers fired 35 shots into the late-model bronze Thunderbird. No officers were injured during the 2 a.m. confrontation in front of the deserted Foothill Boulevard restaurant. The manager, who had been tied up by the robbers and left behind, also was unharmed.

Police said the officers, who are members of the police department's Special Investigations Section, a secretive unit that often conducts surveillance of people suspected of committing a series of crimes, watched the robbery take place but did not move in because of safety reasons.

After the suspects, who were believed to have been involved in a string of fast-food restaurant robberies, got in their car, the SIS officers pulled up, shouted "Police!" and opened fire upon seeing one of the men point a gun at them, police said.

Three pellet guns that appeared to be authentic handguns were found in the car and on one of the suspects after the shooting. Police said it did not appear that any of the pellet guns had been fired.

The police shooting was being investigated by the department's officer-involved shooting unit. Lt. William Hall, head of the unit, said the officers did not violate a year-old department policy that says officers should protect potential crime victims even if it jeopardizes an undercover investigation.

The policy was instituted after police officials reviewed the procedures of the SIS. A *Times* investigation in 1988 found that the 19-member unit often followed violent criminals but did not take advantage of opportunities to arrest them until after robberies or burglaries occurred — in many cases leaving victims terrorized or injured.

Police said the officers involved in Monday's shooting are SIS veterans with an average of 19 years of experience with the Los Angeles Police Department. The officers were identified as Richard Spelman, 39; James Tippings, 48; Gary Strickland, 46; Jerry Brooks, 50; John Helms, 40; Joe Callian, 31; Warren Eggar, 48; Richard Zierenberg, 43; and David Harrison, 41.

The gunfire early Monday echoed throughout the commercial and residential area where apartment buildings sit alongside restaurants, convenience stores and small service shops.

"I woke up hearing many, many shots," said Alejandro Medina, whose corner apartment overlooks the shooting area. "I got up to see and then there were more shots. I hit the floor."

Although SIS officers had watched at least one of the men off and on since the beginning of the year, Hall said the suspects were not seen breaking any laws before they forced their way into the McDonald's at 7950 Foothill Boulevard.

"At the times the surveillance has been on the suspects, [police] saw no crimes," Hall said. "To stop them they needed a reason. That had not occurred. Once [the suspects] went up to the restaurant, maybe they crossed that threshold."

Hall said the officers, however, then decided they did not want to risk the safety of the restaurant manager by attempting to burst into the McDonald's and arrest the robbers.

"The decision was made that, since there never had been any injuries involved in any of these robberies, rather than try to force entry into the building, they would wait and let the suspects exit," Hall said.

The names of the three dead men were not released Monday. The wounded man was identified as Alfredo Olivas, 19, of Hollywood. He was in serious condition, suffering from two shotgun wounds, at Holy Cross Medical Center in Mission Hills. Police said that when he recovers, Olivas will be arrested on a murder charge because, under California law, he can be held responsible for any deaths that occur during a crime he allegedly committed.

Police began their investigation of the suspects after the robbery of a McDonald's in downtown Los Angeles in September, Hall said. Because detectives and McDonald's security officials believed the robbers had knowledge of how the restaurant operated, several employees were questioned and given lie-detector tests.

One employee was fired after failing the polygraph examination but there was no evidence to arrest him, police said. The downtown robbery was similar to at least six others — five at McDonald's restaurants and one at a Carl's Jr. — in Los Angeles since August, police said. In each case, the robbers had knowledge of the business's operations and forced a lone manager at gunpoint to open a safe after hours, police said.

SIS officers began to follow the former employee in early January and, on Sunday night, the officers watched as he met with three other men in Venice and drove with them to Sunland in a bronze Thunderbird belonging to one of the men, police said.

The four men arrived at the McDonald's as it was closing at midnight and watched it from the Thunderbird parked across the street, police said. At 1:36 a.m. when only night manager Robin Cox, 24, was still inside, three of the suspects got out of the Thunderbird and approached the restaurant.

Hall said one man remained in front while two others attempted to break in a rear door. Cox heard the break-in attempt and called police. Patrol units were not dispatched, however, because SIS officers were watching the restaurant.

Hall said the officers held back on arresting the suspects because the suspects were too spread out. As the officers watched, the two suspects at the rear of the restaurant moved to a side door and forced their way into the McDonald's.

All four suspects then entered the restaurant. Cox was tied up and threatened at gunpoint until she opened the restaurant's safe. Several thousand dollars was taken, police said.

The suspects came out of the restaurant half an hour later and walked across the street to the Thunderbird. After they were in the car, four unmarked cars containing eight officers pulled up from behind and one officer ran up on foot.

Hall said the officers identified themselves and were wearing clearly marked "raid" jackets that said "police" on the front and back.

"When they approached the vehicle they saw one of the suspects with a handgun point it toward their direction," Hall said. "One of the officers said, 'Watch out, they've got a gun.'

"At that time we had several officers fire into the vehicle. The passenger in the front exited and fled into an open field. He was carrying a handgun and several officers fired at him. All the shots were fired in just a few seconds."

Hall said that after the firing stopped, two officers approached the car and fired four more shots into it when they saw "two of the suspects were moving around, reaching down to a floorboard where a gun was."

A total of 23 shotgun blasts and 12 shots from 45-caliber handguns were fired by police at the suspected robbers, Hall said.

Several residents in the area said they were awakened by the gunfire and shouts of the police officers.

"My husband yelled to me to call the police," said Ronda Caracci, whose apartment also offers a view of the shooting area. "I looked out the window and said, 'Hey, it is the police.'"

ATTORNEY CALLS SPECIAL LAPD SQUAD 'ASSASSINS' AS CIVIL RIGHTS TRIAL OPENS

Courts: Case will focus on tactics of Special Investigations Officers who fatally shot three robbers.

January 10, 1992

Members of a controversial Los Angeles police squad who fatally shot three men after a 1990 robbery in Sunland were called "assassins with badges" Thursday by an attorney representing the families of the dead men in a civil rights lawsuit.

Attorney Stephen Yagman made the allegation during opening statements in a U.S. District Court trial that will focus on the tactics of the police department's Special Investigations Section, a 19-member surveillance unit that targets suspects in serious crimes.

The families of the three men killed in the Feb. 12, 1990, shooting, along with a fourth robber who was shot but survived, charge that the SIS is a "death squad" that follows suspects, allows them to commit crimes and then frequently shoots them when officers move in to make arrests.

"What they do is attempt to terminate the existence of the people they are following," Yagman told the 10 jurors hearing the case.

Deputy City Atty. Don Vincent countered that the officers acted properly and that the SIS is a valuable police tool. "This is a necessary organization that most police departments have," he said. "It is even more important in Los Angeles, a city of 365 square miles . . . where the criminals are just as mobile as the police."

The trial before Judge J. Spencer Letts is expected to last at least two weeks. The suit names members of the SIS, Police Chief Daryl F. Gates, Mayor Tom Bradley, the Police Commission and all former commissioners and chiefs during the unit's 25-year existence. Yagman says officials have allowed an environment in which a "shadowy" unit such as the SIS can operate. The shooting in front of a McDonald's restaurant on Foothill Boulevard occurred after a lengthy investigation into a series of restaurant robberies. Police said that in late 1989 investigators identified the suspects — Jesus Arango, 25, and Herbert Burgos, 37, of Venice and Juan Bahena, 20, and Alfredo Olivas, 21, both of Hollywood.

SIS officers followed the four intermittently for three months before they watched them break into the

McDonald's where manager Robin L. Cox was working alone after closing for the night.

After they tied up, gagged and blindfolded Cox, the robbers left the restaurant with $14,000 from its safe.

When all four were seated in their getaway car, SIS officers moved in on foot and in cars. Police said two of the men pointed guns at the officers, who opened fire, killing three and wounding Olivas in the stomach. Police said they recovered three pellet guns that resembled pistols.

Officers later explained that they could not make arrests before the robbery because the four men moved too quickly and were too spread out around the restaurant.

Whether the men in the car were armed at the time of the shooting will be at issue in the trial. Yagman said they had no weapons and were shot in the back.

Olivas, the first witness to testify, said that the robbers stored their weapons in the trunk of the car before getting in. The shooting started a few seconds later, said Olivas, who is serving a 17-year prison term for the robberies.

Vincent in his opening statement sharply disagreed, saying two of the robbers drew the police fire when they pointed their weapons at the officers. "Officers have a right to self-defense," he said. "They don't have to wait for someone to shoot them."

FBI PROBES SLAYING OF ROBBERS BY LAPD

Police: Existence of inquiry came to light in suit over SIS unit's killings of three men who had robbed a Valley restaurant.

January 16, 1992

The FBI is investigating the killing of three robbers in Sunland by a controversial Los Angeles police squad, and the Justice Department apparently has taken the case before a federal grand jury, court documents showed Wednesday.

The investigation surfaced when the U.S. Attorney's Office mentioned it in asking a U.S. district judge to throw out a subpoena for an FBI agent called to testify in the trial of a lawsuit filed over the shooting.

The request indicated that the shooting by the Special Investigations Section had been under investigation for nearly a year.

The FBI agent, Richard Boeh, was subpoenaed to testify in the civil rights suit filed after the Feb. 12, 1990, incident, when nine SIS officers fired at a getaway car used by four robbers who had just held up a McDonald's restaurant in Sunland. They killed three and wounded the fourth.

The survivor and relatives of the slain men are suing the city and the police department, alleging that the SIS squad violated the robbers' civil rights by executing them without cause.

Police have contended in testimony in the week-old trial of the lawsuit that the robbers were shot because they pointed pistols at the officers. Weapons found at the scene were discovered to be pellet pistols, similar in appearance to firearms.

Stephen Yagman, the attorney representing the plaintiffs, summoned Boeh as a witness, saying the federal agent has information that could be vital to proving the suit's key contention — that the robbers had placed their pellet guns in the trunk of the getaway car before getting into it, and therefore were unarmed when the SIS officers surprised them and opened fire.

Yagman said the FBI investigation dates from early last year, when Boeh interviewed the sole surviving robber, Alfredo Olivas, now 21 and serving a 17-year prison term for robbery.

"It would be a perversion of justice for the jury to deliberate this case without hearing what the FBI has found," Yagman said outside of court.

But the U.S. Attorney's Office filed a motion to quash the subpoena for Boeh. In a declaration contained in the motion, Boeh said he has been investigating the police shooting since April 1991 and indicated that he has provided testimony to a grand jury investigating the incident.

"If called to testify, my testimony would violate the rule of secrecy relating to proceedings before the grand jury," Boeh said.

Boeh said that if he testified he would also have to reveal the identity of informants and other details of the federal investigation.

"To my knowledge, the information from the informants and the identity of the informants is known only to the government," Boeh said. "My testimony would reveal facts relating to the strategy of the government in the investigation."

Assistant U.S. Atty. Sean Berry, who is seeking to block Boeh's testimony, did not return a phone call seeking comment. The U.S. Attorney's Office routinely withholds comment on grand jury proceedings, which are secret.

Los Angeles Deputy City Atty. Don Vincent, who is representing the police officers and other defendants in the civil rights suit, including Police Chief Daryl F. Gates and Mayor Tom Bradley, could not be reached for comment after the trial recessed Wednesday.

Judge J. Spencer Letts has not yet ruled on whether Yagman will be able to call Boeh to testify.

In trial testimony Wednesday, a parade of former top managers of the police department testified briefly about their roles in running the department — some going back to the early 1960s.

Yagman called 13 former members of the civilian Police Commission and three former police chiefs in an attempt to bolster the lawsuit's contention that the SIS, a secretive unit that places criminal suspects under surveillance, is a "death squad" that has operated for 25 years because commissioners and chiefs have exercised little control over the department.

According to testimony, the unit has been involved in 45 shootings since 1965, killing 28 people and wounding 27.

Most of the former commissioners testified that they considered the appointed post a part-time job, and four testified they never knew of the SIS while they were members of the commission. Former Chief Tom Reddin, who held the top job from 1967 to 1969, said in brief testimony that he had known of the unit's existence but had never investigated its activities.

Roger Murdock, who served as interim chief for six months in 1969, said he thought the SIS unit was formed to investigate the assassination of Sen. Robert F. Kennedy.

Yagman did not ask Sen. Ed Davis (R-Santa Clarita), who was police chief from 1969 to 1978, about the SIS. Instead, he asked how Davis viewed the role of the Police Commission during his time as chief.

"I might have been wrong but I always thought they were my bosses," Davis said. "They were tough bosses. . . . I danced to their tune. I wanted to keep my job for a while."

NOTE: FBI Agent Richard Boeh refused to testify about his investigation of the SIS and was held in contempt of court. The agent immediately appealed and the contempt order was reversed by the 9th Circuit Court of Appeals. The trial then resumed after a month's delay without his testimony.

CHRISTOPHER REPORT: IT CUTS BOTH WAYS

Courts: The findings of the city-commissioned panel could work against L.A. when jurors rule in police brutality suits.

February 4, 1992

As Mayor Tom Bradley sat in the witness chair, a thin smile played on his face. He was facing an uneasy situation that he and the city may have to get used to.

Bradley was testifying in federal court last month as a defendant in a civil rights trial. And he was repeatedly saying, yes, he fully agreed with the conclusions of the Christopher Commission, the independent, blue-ribbon panel that last year investigated the Los Angeles Police Department and found problems with management, excessive force and racism.

"You have no reservations about your agreement with those conclusions?" the plaintiffs' attorney, Stephen Yagman, asked.

CRIME BEAT

"No," Bradley told the 10 jurors.

Bradley was testifying in a civil rights case in which police officers are accused of killing three robbery suspects without provocation. Police managers and Bradley are also accused in the suit of tolerating excessive force and many of the departmental problems cited by the commission.

In effect, the mayor was being cut with his own sword; after all, he was a main force behind creation of the commission. Now, the commission's findings could prove pivotal when jurors decide if the officers acted improperly and their supervisors — right up to Bradley and Chief Daryl F. Gates — are responsible.

While the trial is the first in which the report has been brought up by plaintiffs against police and city officials, it most likely will not be the last.

Yagman, a civil rights attorney who specializes in police-related lawsuits, said he has clients with five more cases set for trial this year. He plans in each case to introduce the commission report as evidence of a police department that he says is out of control. Other civil rights attorneys said last week that they plan to do the same.

"It is paradoxical and sweet," Yagman said of having such a key document essentially prepared for him by the city that his clients are suing. "The effect of having this report is like putting whipped cream on a malt."

Meantime, Deputy City Atty. Don Vincent, in charge of defending the city against police-related lawsuits, said

97

his staff is developing strategies to deal with the report when it comes up in trials. He conceded that his task may only be beginning.

"It is a valuable tool for all civil rights attorneys," Vincent said. "I am sure we will be facing this for several years to come."

Though the report has been discussed at length in front of the jury in the trial, Vincent hopes to block inclusion of the 228-page volume as evidence in the case. Though pointing out that the report makes many favorable conclusions about the police department, Vincent said its damaging claims are largely hearsay and opinion — not evidence.

The current case arose from a shooting on Feb. 12, 1990, in which nine members of the police Special Investigations Section opened fire on four suspects who had just left a McDonald's restaurant in Sunland after a holdup. All four men were hit by police shots and only one survived.

The families of the dead men and the survivor, who was later imprisoned for robbery, filed suit against the officers, Bradley, Gates and the Police Commission alleging that the robbers' civil rights were violated because the police opened fire without provocation. The lawsuit also alleges that the SIS is a "death squad" that has been created and fostered by an environment of lax management, brutality and racism in the department.

More than a year later, the Christopher Commission, formed by Bradley after the outcry that accompanied the Rodney G. King beating, delivered a report highly critical of management of the department and concluded that the police force had problems with excessive force, racism and a "code of silence" among its officers.

Yagman said in a recent interview that many of the report's conclusions mirror the allegations in the lawsuit spawned by the McDonald's shooting.

He unsuccessfully sought to have Warren Christopher, who chaired the commission, testify as a witness. However, U.S. District Judge J. Spencer Letts has allowed Yagman to use the commission's report to question witnesses such as Bradley, Gates and police commissioners.

Letts is expected to rule later whether the report will be accepted as evidence and whether jurors will be able to refer to it during deliberations.

Regardless of the ruling, the report and its conclusions are already a large part of the trial record. So much so that at one point during Bradley's testimony, Letts interrupted and cautioned the jury that they were not deciding a case on the incident that prompted the report.

"Don't get confused," Letts said. "Rodney King is not here."

Outside of court, Yagman has told reporters that his questioning of witnesses has covered "every single chapter" of the report.

But how important the Christopher Commission report will be to the case and others that follow cannot be determined until verdicts are returned.

Jurors in the McDonald's case have heard conflicting testimony over the report. Bradley said he agreed with the report's conclusions, while Gates testified that he believes many of them are untrue or exaggerated.

And even in testifying that he accepted the report, Bradley sought to repair any damage to the defense by stressing that the report targets only a small portion of the force. He said that, overall, the city has the finest big-city police department in the country.

But Yagman and other attorneys said the commission report will automatically lend a strong degree of validation to claims made in lawsuits of police abuse.

"This is not a wild-eyed civil rights lawyer saying this, it is a blue-ribbon panel appointed to fairly evaluate the LAPD," attorney Benjamin Schonbrun said. He plans to introduce the report as evidence in two upcoming trials against the Los Angeles police.

"I've been saying these same things for years," Yagman said of the report's conclusions. "Everybody now believes it."

Other attorneys specializing in police misconduct litigation said the effect that the report will have on how they prepare lawsuits against the Los Angeles police will be significant, and possibly expensive as damages are assessed.

"By all means, it is terribly important," said Hugh R. Manes, a civil rights lawyer in Los Angeles for more than 35 years. "I think it is a very important tool against the LAPD. It is based upon their own files and records going back 10 years and thus shows a pattern of misconduct."

Manes said the report's broad coverage of the department's problems will mean that at least portions of the report will be relevant, and admissible, in almost all LAPD-related cases.

Veteran police litigator Donald Cook has a federal suit pending against Gates and the city that also alleges misconduct by the SIS.

"And guess what I am going to use as evidence?" he asked recently.

He said that, like Yagman, he will attempt to introduce the commission's report as evidence of the department's poor management and condoning of excessive force.

"It is a great piece of evidence — really trustworthy, credible evidence of what we have been saying for years," Cook said of the report. "It is ironic that we are validated by the city. It is really ironic.

"I think the city is getting a dose of justice."

Vincent, the deputy city attorney, has yet to mount the city's defense in the current case. Though he declined to reveal specifics about his strategy, he said his task is to clearly separate the report from the facts of the shooting that is the basis for the lawsuit.

"We are going to stick to the facts of the case," Vincent said. "Our opinion is like the mayor's. It is still the finest police department in the nation."

He said that almost all documents used as evidence in lawsuits against the police come from police-shooting reports, policy statements and disciplinary records. So facing the commission report is not a totally unfamiliar situation. Still, Vincent said, its impact may be the most difficult to deal with.

"I think it is significant," he said. "It has certainly gotten recognition and prestige.

"But I think it is something we will effectively deal with. We think some of it is flawed. It gives a skewed view."

That view comes from the report's focus on problems within the department without a full reporting on positive aspects of the force, Vincent said. The report's conclusions are too broadly drawn, he added, and jurors will be unable to ascribe them to the officers involved in the McDonald's shooting because neither they nor their unit is mentioned in the report.

"This type of information should never be used," Vincent said. "It has come into this case to prejudice officers that are not even named in it."

Still, Vincent is resigned to having that task of deflecting the effect of the report in trials to come.

"I am not sure of all the ways it can be used against us," he said. "So we are thinking about it.

"We are just going to take it one case at a time."

L.A. DETECTIVE TELLS DETAILS OF FATAL SHOOTING

Civil rights: The officer is testifying as a defendant in a suit alleging the Special Investigations Section killed three unarmed robbers.

March 5, 1992

In testimony lasting nearly three hours in federal court Wednesday, a Los Angeles police officer described in grim detail the shooting in which he and fellow officers fired 35 times at four robbers outside a Sunland McDonald's, killing three and wounding the fourth.

Detective John Helms said he fired six times with a shotgun and three times with a pistol after seeing one of the bandits flee the getaway car with a gun and a second man brandishing a gun inside the car.

Afterward, police discovered that the weapons used by the robbers during the Feb. 12, 1990, incident were pellet guns that were replicas of real firearms.

During the shooting, Helms said: "I was looking for any indication that these men were trying to submit to arrest. I saw nothing" that indicated surrender.

Helms' testimony came in the months-long trial of a civil rights lawsuit filed by the surviving robber and the families of the men killed.

Their suit contends that the nine officers who opened fire did so without warning or provocation and that the use of excessive force violated their rights. The suit says the officers, all members of the department's Special Investigations Section, are part of a "death squad" that specifically targets criminal suspects for execution.

The surviving robber, Alfredo Olivas, testified earlier that the bandits had stowed their pellet guns in the trunk of the car after the robbery and therefore were unarmed when fired upon. Several officers later testified briefly that they saw guns being brandished, prompting the shooting.

Now, in the defense phase of the trial, the officers are testifying at length about the incident and why they opened fire.

Seemingly choked with emotion during some of his testimony about the shooting, Helms told jurors that, because of tactical and safety concerns, the officers could not move in to arrest the bandits until the thieves left the McDonald's after robbing the lone employee inside.

When the four men were in their car, which was parked on the street, four SIS cars moved in to block their escape. Two of the police cars actually hit the getaway car, "jamming" it behind a parked truck.

As officers jumped out of their cars, Helms said, he heard one officer shout "Gun!" — a warning that he saw a gun in the getaway car. Helms then heard shots being fired and shouts of "Police! You're under arrest!"

"Things were going on simultaneously," Helms said. "I saw a man get out . . . and I saw a gun in his right hand. I saw him start to run."

Helms said that, because the robbers had used guns during previous crimes, he believed the men still inside the car were also armed and that the officers surrounding the car were in danger.

"I started directing fire at the back," Helms said. "The next thing I saw was one of the handguns being brandished through one of the holes in the rear window."

Helms fired again, emptying his shotgun of shells. In the meantime, other officers shot the man who had run from the car when he allegedly turned and pointed a pellet gun at them.

"I knew I was out of ammo on my shotgun," Helms said. "I put it in my car and took out my .45."

Helms then described how he and his partner approached the car to make sure the three robbers inside were no longer a threat. He said that when he looked into the car one of the men in the backseat was reaching for a gun on the floor. Helms said he yelled for the man to stop and fired twice when he did not comply. Helms said the other man in the backseat then reached for the weapon, and Helms fired at him as well.

Helms said he did not know how long the shooting lasted. "When I believe my life is in danger, I am not a good estimator of time," he said.

During cross-examination of Helms, the plaintiffs' attorney, Stephen Yagman, pointed out that the weapon the officer claimed to have seen in the car was an unloaded pellet gun. Yagman has said that the jury will have to decide whether it is plausible that the robbers would have pointed or attempted to reach for pellet guns when confronted by nine officers with shotguns and .45s.

GATES WANTS TO BE 'JUDGE, JURY, EXECUTIONER,' LAWYER SAYS

Courts: Attorneys make their closing arguments in the trial stemming from a February 1990 shooting in Sunland in which officers killed three robbers.

March 25, 1992

The Los Angeles Police Department is a "Frankenstein monster" created by Chief Daryl F. Gates, who has allowed a squad of officers to operate as "assassins," a federal jury was told Tuesday in a trial over a police shooting that left three robbers dead.

But the allegations made by an attorney representing the robbers and their families was rebutted by the city's attorney, who defended Gates and said members of the police squad — the Special Investigations Section — use tactics designed to avoid shootings.

The statements came during closing arguments in a three-month trial stemming from the Feb. 12, 1990, shooting outside a McDonald's restaurant in Sunland.

"The police have gone too far in Los Angeles by using excessive force," plaintiffs' attorney Stephen Yagman said.

"The LAPD and Daryl Gates have ruled this community for 14 years by fear," Yagman said. "He does and has done as he pleases. The LAPD is his Frankenstein monster. It is something that has gone beyond all bounds. . . . He wants to be judge, jury and executioner."

Gates and nine SIS officers are defendants in the lawsuit filed by the families of three bandits who were killed by police and a fourth who was shot but survived. The lawsuit contends that the officers used excessive force and fired on the robbers without cause. The 10-member jury is expected to begin deliberations today.

Deputy City Atty. Don Vincent countered Yagman's claims by telling jurors that evidence presented in the case clearly shows the nine officers opened fire when they sensed they were in imminent danger. He defended the firepower — 35 shots from shotguns and handguns — as being an appropriate response when the officers saw the robbers brandishing weapons. The weapons were later discovered to be pellet guns resembling real handguns.

Vincent cautioned jurors not to confuse the superior firepower of police with excessive force, noting that each officer feared for his life and had reason to fire. "This is not the Old West where you get out on the street and have a shootout at noon," Vincent said. "They are not the sitting ducks of the public."

According to trial testimony, the officers opened fire on the bandits after they watched them break into the closed McDonald's, rob the lone employee inside and then return to their getaway car. The shooting started almost immediately when officers converged on the car.

The plaintiffs contend that the bandits had put their unloaded pellet guns in the trunk of the car and therefore were unarmed when the shooting started.

Noting that U.S. District Judge J. Spencer Letts ruled earlier that the police had probable cause to arrest the four suspects before the robbery, Yagman argued that the officers allowed the crime to take place and orchestrated the stakeout in such a way that the shooting was "inevitable, inescapable." He said the special police unit has a long record of using tactics that often end in shootings.

Yagman said police took the pellet guns from the trunk after the shooting and "planted" one inside the car and one on the body of a robber who had run from the car before being shot by police. He said police photos show the gun inside the car in different positions, indicating police tampered with the evidence.

He said that while the claim that guns were planted might be "hard to digest," the alternative — the police story — defies common sense.

"What person, when faced with nine officers with shotguns, would point an unloaded, inoperable pellet gun at them?" he asked. "What does common sense tell you?"

In his closing argument, Vincent denied that Gates condones excessive force. He also said an extensive department investigation cleared the officers of any wrongdoing.

He recounted police testimony that the gun was indeed moved. Vincent said the gun was photographed as it was found by officers and then removed from the car but later replaced so additional photos could be taken. But the original photographs are clearly marked, he said.

Vincent noted that the weapon allegedly planted on the body of Herbert Burgos was the same weapon the survivor, Alfredo Olivas, testified that Burgos used during the robbery. Vincent asked jurors how the officers could have known on which robber to plant which weapon.

"Nothing was planted in that car," he said. "It would mean that it was happenstance that they placed the right gun with the right body."

Vincent said the explanation for why the robbers pointed unloaded pellet guns at the police will never be known. "They might have thought it was someone else and raised the guns to scare them," he said.

NOTE: The federal jury hearing the SIS case found for the plaintiffs, awarding the families of the killed robbers and the lone survivor a total of $44,042 in damages.

COUNCIL SUED OVER FATAL
POLICE SHOOTING

Attorney offers to drop members as defendants if they make Gates pay damages assessed in same incident. Officials angrily charge extortion.

April 2, 1992

Los Angeles city council members were sued Wednesday over a police shooting that left three robbers dead, but the attorney who filed the case offered to drop them as defendants if they make Police Chief Daryl F. Gates personally pay for damages assessed against him this week for the same shooting.

Council members familiar with the new suit and a city attorney who defends the city in police-related cases reacted angrily to the offer from civil rights attorney Stephen Yagman, which was contained in a letter to the council that accompanied the new $20-million suit.

"Sounds like extortion, doesn't it?" said Deputy City Atty. Don Vincent, head of the city's police litigation unit.

Councilman Zev Yaroslavsky, who favors making Gates pay the damages from his own pocket, said he was nonetheless disturbed by Yagman's letter.

"Nobody likes to be threatened," he said.

Councilwoman Joy Picus, who is undecided on the issue of whether Gates should pay, said Yagman was using tactics of intimidation and harassment.

"The nerve of him," she said. "I've dealt with attorneys who have tried to extort and threaten me before. I'll be damned if I'll be intimidated by him."

Yagman denied his offer to the council was improper or threatening.

"Everybody has a right to ask people in the government to do or not do something, and to say if you do it the way we want we will take action or refrain from taking action," Yagman said. "That's not extortion. That is trying to settle the lawsuit."

The lawsuit filed Wednesday in U.S. District Court against the council and numerous police officers and officials is the latest twist in the case that has followed the Feb. 12, 1990, shooting outside a McDonald's restaurant in Sunland.

The shooting initially spawned a lawsuit on behalf of four family members of three robbers killed by members of the police Special Investigations Section and a fourth robber who was shot but survived.

The plaintiffs, represented by Yagman, contended that the police used excessive force and fired on the robbers without provocation. Gates was named as defendant because the suit said he was ultimately responsible for the officers' actions and condoned the use of excessive force.

After a three-month trial, a federal jury returned a verdict in favor of the plaintiffs Monday and awarded punitive damages of $44,042 against Gates and nine members of the SIS. Jurors said the damage award was purposely set low because they believed the chief and his officers should pay it out of their own pockets. Gates was to pay $20,505 of the award.

The verdict touched off a debate this week among council members over whether the city should pay the damages anyway. The council has routinely picked up the tab for punitive damages assessed against police officers for incidents that occurred while they were on the job.

On Wednesday, the new lawsuit further added to the controversy. The new suit is identical to the first one but was filed on behalf of two-year-old Johanna Trevino, daughter of Juan Bahena, one of the robbers police killed.

Yagman said Trevino was born six days after Bahena, whose real name was Javier Trevino, was killed and can file the lawsuit under a federal precedent set last year in another case involving the SIS. In that case, in which Yagman is also the plaintiff's attorney, a federal appeals court held that a child who was not yet born when a parent was killed by police may still sue for damages over losing a parent.

The new lawsuit names 20 SIS officers, Gates, Mayor Tom Bradley, 17 former police chiefs and commission members and all city council members in office at the time of the shooting.

In a letter enclosed with the suit to the council, Yagman said:

"If the council votes not to indemnify Gates for the punitive damages in this case, then all of you who make up the majority so voting will be dismissed voluntarily as defendants in this new case."

Vincent, the city attorney, said he could not comment on the lawsuit until he received it. But of Yagman's letter to the council, he said, "I have never heard of an attorney doing anything like that at all."

Council members who received it Wednesday also reacted strongly.

Councilwoman Joan Mike Flores said the lawsuit and Yagman's tactics were an outrage.

"I will not be intimidated by these types of tactics," she said in a statement.

Yaroslavsky said the letter Yagman sent could hinder efforts by council members who believe Gates should pay the damages awarded by the jury.

"I don't think Yagman's letter advances that cause at all," he said. "I think it's unnecessary and inappropriate. My inclination is not to pay for Chief Gates. . . . I will come to a final conclusion based on the facts, not a threat."

But Yagman said his letter was an effort to make the council abide by the wishes of the jury that heard the McDonald's shooting case.

"We are just saying that if they refuse to indemnify Gates, we will drop the case," Yagman said. "It might be wrong to threaten to sue them. But we haven't done that.

We have sued them and said, 'If you act in a responsible way we will consider dismissing you from this lawsuit.'"

ATTORNEYS AWARDED FEE OF $378,000 IN BRUTALITY SUIT

Courts: The ruling could lead to more sparks between lawyer and the city council.

August 5, 1992

A federal judge has awarded $378,000 in legal fees to civil rights attorney Stephen Yagman and his partners for their work on a successful excessive-force lawsuit against former Los Angeles Police Chief Daryl Gates and nine police officers.

The ruling released Tuesday sets up another potential conflict in a running legal battle between Yagman and the city council over the council's financial support for officers defending themselves from civil suits alleging brutality.

Yagman outraged city officials earlier this year when he submitted a bill that asked for nearly $1 million in fees for himself and two partners who handled the lawsuit over a 1990 police shooting that left three robbers dead and one wounded outside a McDonald's restaurant in Sunland.

City attorneys, who had argued that the fee award should be about $216,000, said they considered it a victory that Yagman received much less than he asked for, but Yagman said he was satisfied with the amount. A decision has not been made by the city on whether to appeal the decision. After a three-month trial, the surviving robber and the families of the three dead men won a $44,000 damage award against Gates and the nine officers, all members of the department's Special Investigations Section. The plaintiffs maintained that the officers violated the robbers' civil rights by opening fire on them without cause, and that Gates' leadership fostered such excessive force.

The determination of legal fees by U.S. District Judge J. Spencer Letts on Friday could widen the battle between Yagman and the council over who will pay the lawyers' fees. Although the jury had urged that Gates and the officers pay the $44,000 damages personally, the council earlier this year voted to pay the awards from the city treasury.

Yagman said Tuesday that the legal fees awarded in the case should also be personally paid by Gates and the officers. Under federal law, an attorney who brings a successful civil rights case to trial must be paid by the defendants, with a judge determining the amount after hearing arguments from both sides.

"We have no judgment against the city," Yagman said. "We have a judgment against nine SIS officers and Gates. They should pay it. Why should the taxpayers pay?"

Yagman said that if the council pays the $378,000 from city coffers, it will provide him with new ammunition in another lawsuit stemming from the same police shooting.

The second case, filed on behalf of a daughter of one of the dead robbers, names council members as defendants as well as the police. Yagman argued that council members should be held responsible for the officers' actions on the grounds that their decision to pay the damages in the first case in effect condoned the police misconduct that the jury found.

Yagman has contended that each time the council members vote to shield police officers from personal financial penalties in civil brutality suits they strengthen his argument that they are promoting police brutality and should also be personally liable for damages.

The second case has not yet been scheduled for trial. But Letts last week refused to dismiss the council members as defendants, rejecting the city attorney's argument that they are automatically immune from civil liability for their official actions.

Deputy City Atty. Annette Keller said council members don't have a choice over whether to pay such fees.

"It is part of the legal obligation of the city to defend employees sued for action taken in the course and scope of their employment," Keller said. "We are obligated to pay any judgment for attorney fees. It is not an issue for the council."

Yagman said his proposed fee was simply a "wish list"

and that he was pleased with Letts' ruling. "This is a lot of money and I am happy to get it," Yagman said. In a 24-page order outlining his decision on fees, Letts praised Yagman for taking on the case that he characterized as "peculiarly undesirable" because the plaintiffs were a convicted robber and the families of robbers.

A *Times* investigation of the SIS four years ago spawned criticism that members of the unit trailing people with long criminal records often watched violent crimes take place without making a move to stop them so that the criminals could be arrested on the most serious charges possible, carrying more severe sentences.

In the McDonald's case, members of the unit followed the robbers to the restaurant and watched as they broke in and robbed the lone employee inside. She was left physically unhurt but is also suing the officers, claiming that the incident was handled negligently.

KILLED BY A KID

ROOKIE OFFICER DIES IN STRUGGLE FOR GUN

Suspect, 16, killed.

LOS ANGELES TIMES
June 8, 1988

A ROOKIE Los Angeles police officer, on street patrol less than three months, was fatally shot Tuesday during a struggle for his gun with a 16-year-old burglary suspect he confronted on a North Hollywood street, police said.

The teen-age gunman, Robert Steele of North Holly-wood, was later tracked by police dogs to the attic of a nearby vacant house, where he was shot to death by four officers after he repeatedly attempted to reach for the re-volver he had taken from the slain police officer, Cmdr. William Booth said.

A 19-year-old accomplice in the burglary was cap-tured, police said.

Officer James Beyea, 24, was pronounced dead at 1:28 a.m. at St. Joseph Medical Center in Burbank, less than an hour after he was shot in the head and leg, apparently with his own gun, Booth said.

Beyea and Officer Ignacio Gonzalez, 44, an 18-year veteran who was Beyea's training officer, had answered a 12:20 a.m. burglary alarm call at an electronics store at 7261 Lankershim Blvd.

Door Open

When the officers arrived at Alpha Electronics, Booth said, they found a door open and went inside to search. They found no one in the store but could not search one storage room that had been locked from the inside.

Shortly after they walked outside to wait for the owner of the business, who had a key to the storage room, the burglar alarm went off again and the officers saw one person running from the rear of the building.

They quickly returned to their patrol car and drove around the block in an attempt to cut the suspect off, Booth said.

"Then they split up," the police spokesman said. "Beyea went on foot and Gonzalez stayed in the car. They thought this would be the best way to go after the suspect."

Beyea caught up with the suspect on Hinds Avenue, just north of Wyandotte Street — about two blocks from the electronics store — and attempted to arrest him, Booth said. From the car, Gonzalez saw his partner and the suspect struggling for control of a gun.

Heard Gunfire

"Gonzalez was about a block away when he saw the struggle," Booth said. "As he went toward them, he heard and saw gunfire."

Beyea fell to the ground, Booth said, and the suspect fired at Gonzalez as he approached. Gonzalez returned the fire, but neither was hit. The suspect then ran off while Gonzalez went to Beyea's aid.

About 50 officers, assisted by a helicopter and seven police dogs, searched a 16-block area around the shooting site, Booth said. About 4:30 a.m., one of the dogs led officers to a vacant house at 11828 Runnymede St., about three blocks from where Beyea had been shot.

Officers entered the one-story house, located on a wooded lot, and found Steele hiding in a corner of the attic.

According to a police statement, Sgt. Gary Nanson, 34, and Officer John Hall, 41, climbed into the attic and ordered Steele to raise his hands. The teen-ager complied and told the officers that the man they wanted was hiding downstairs, police said, but then he reached to his side to grab a gun.

Hall fired one time and wounded Steele in the head, police said. Despite several warnings to stay still, Steele twice again attempted to pick the gun up and was fatally shot by Nanson and two other officers, who had also climbed into the attic, the statement said.

The gun retrieved from Steele's side was Beyea's service revolver, Booth said. Ballistics tests will be conducted to determine if it was the weapon used to kill the officer, he said.

No other weapon was found, police said, and no one else was found in the house.

But during a search of the area, officers found Alberto Hernandez, 19, hiding in bushes about a block from where Beyea was killed. He admitted taking part in the burglary and was arrested on suspicion of murder, police said.

1st Death This Year

Beyea was the first Los Angeles police officer killed in the line of duty this year. Two were killed last year.

Beyea, a Reseda resident, entered the Police Academy last October and graduated March 25. Capt. Charles (Rick) Dinse, commander of the North Hollywood Division, where the rookie was assigned, said Beyea was routinely paired with a veteran who had training officer qualifications.

"I can only say he was considered by his supervisors and training officer to be one of our best," Dinse said. "He was a sharp policeman who we expected to have a great career."

Beyea, who was single, was born in Reseda and graduated from Cleveland High School in 1981. He served in the Air Force and Air Force Reserve.

Beyea's grandfather was a Los Angeles traffic officer before retiring in 1961, police said.

Funeral arrangements were pending Tuesday. Beyea is survived by his mother, Cathleen Beyea of Northridge. Beyea is the second North Hollywood officer to be killed in three years. Detective Thomas C. Williams, 42, was shot to death Oct. 31, 1985, in what authorities said was an effort to prevent him from testifying in a robbery case.

Times staff writer Steve Padilla contributed to this report.

DEATH FOR DEATH

Youth had minor scrapes with law but didn't fit image of a cop killer.

June 9, 1988

Bobby Steele was swinging the bat well, and by Sunday was on a nine-game hitting streak with a city youth league baseball team, the Sun Valley Park Pirates.

On Monday, the 16-year-old was able to parlay a morning dental appointment into a whole day off from school. The grandparents who raised him didn't mind that he spent the rest of the day around the house.

But by 9 p.m. he was ready to get out of the North Hollywood home where he had lived his entire life. He baked himself a batch of cookies and then left to meet a friend. When he walked out the door, he left behind everything that appeared to be routine about his life.

A few hours later and a few blocks away, Robert Jay Steele killed a cop, Los Angeles police say. A few hours after that, police killed him.

"It doesn't make sense," his grandmother, Pauline Steele, said Wednesday as she sat on the dead youth's bed and looked at the collection of baseball trophies on his bureau.

"It seems like we are talking about two separate people," said his sister, Lori Lyn Steele. To his family, Steele may have been a mischievous youth, someone who had his troubles in school and with authorities, but he did not fit the picture of a cop killer.

At 12:20 a.m. Tuesday, however, according to police, the teen-ager grappled with a rookie police officer for control of the officer's gun. Within seconds, Officer James Beyea, 24, fell to the ground, fatally shot in the head.

Cornered and Killed

Steele, suspected of having just burglarized a nearby electronics store, then fired the weapon at the policeman's approaching partner and ran off. He was later cornered in the attic of a vacant home and shot to death by officers when, according to authorities, he repeatedly tried to pick up the gun.

"He had been in trouble before but never anything like this," his 23-year-old sister said. "I feel that what happened was that he was scared. He got in with the wrong people, did something wrong and got scared."

Police declined to say whether Steele had a juvenile record. His family said he had minor scrapes with authorities in the last year, including a fight with a teacher and an arrest when a police officer found a pair of brass knuckles in a car in which he was riding. Details of the incidents were unavailable Wednesday.

Steele was a student at North Hollywood High School, where he frequently missed classes, until May 9, administrators said. Then he was placed in a school program supervised by Los Angeles county juvenile authorities, but officials declined to say what prompted the transfer.

"He liked sports and to goof around. But there was a little bit of a mystery about him," said Ricardo Davis, recreation leader at Sun Valley Park, who knew Steele for eight years. "He came to the park right before his games and he left right after. I don't know if the friends he had on the team were his really close friends or just friends while he was here."

Police said a friend away from the park was Alberto Hernandez, 19, of North Hollywood. After Steele left his home Monday night, investigators said, he and Hernandez broke into Alpha Electronics, about six blocks from Steele's home.

A burglar alarm touched off at 12:20 a.m. Tuesday brought Officer Beyea and his partner, Officer Ignacio Gonzalez, to the shop. After searching the premises, they saw someone running away and gave chase.

The officers split up, Beyea on foot and Gonzalez in the car. Soon after, Gonzalez saw Beyea struggling with someone in the street, police said. From a block away, he heard two gunshots and saw his partner fall.

Steele then exchanged gunfire with Gonzalez, police said, and ran through the neighborhood to an abandoned house. A police dog tracked him there at 4:30 a.m.

Police said the K-9 officer, Jon Hall, and Sgt. Gary Nanson, one of dozens of policemen who by then were searching for the suspect, took a ladder from the garage of the vacant home, propped it in the attic entrance in the hallway ceiling and climbed up.

Using flashlights, they spotted Steele between two rafters near a corner of the attic. Steele began to comply with an order to surrender and told the officers that another suspect was in the house, police said, but then suddenly attempted to grab a gun that was by his side. Hall fired once, hitting Steele in the face.

According to police, Hall and Nanson crawled over to Steele and, after examining him, believed that he was dead. They left the gun next to him and backed away so the scene would be undisturbed for investigators.

Police said Hall then climbed out of the attic to search the house. About three minutes after the first shot, police said, Steele stirred and reached for the weapon again despite a warning from Nanson.

Nanson fired his gun, hitting Steele in the face again, police said. Two other officers heard the second shot and quickly climbed into the attic, police said, and both fired their guns when they saw Steele still grabbing for the gun. One shot hit Steele in the face for the third time and the other shot missed.

The officers found Beyea's service revolver at the dead youth's side.

Hernandez, who was found hiding in some bushes nearby, is scheduled to be arraigned today on a murder charge.

A funeral with full police honors is scheduled at 11 a.m. Friday for Beyea, the grandson of a traffic officer, at the Praiswater Funeral Home in Van Nuys, with interment to follow at Oakwood Memorial Park.

1,000 ATTEND RITES FOR SLAIN ROOKIE OFFICER

June 11, 1988

The first police funeral attended by March graduates of the Los Angeles Police Academy was for one of their own.

Two dozen members of the class, tears streaking many of their faces, stood at attention in a line of blue uniforms Friday and snapped crisp salutes as taps was played for Officer James Clark Beyea at Oakwood Memorial Park in Chatsworth.

Beyea, 24, who graduated with them on March 25, was fatally shot about 1:30 a.m. Tuesday in North Hollywood during a struggle for control of his service revolver with a burglary suspect.

His funeral drew about 1,000 mourners, most from law enforcement agencies throughout Southern California. Also in attendance were Beyea's family, Mayor Tom Bradley, Police Chief Daryl F. Gates and representatives of the Air National Guard unit to which Beyea belonged.

'Hurts to Lose Him'

"It hurts to lose him," said Officer William Casey, one of Beyea's academy classmates. "It hurts when anyone in this profession is killed, but when it is someone that you feel is like a member of your family, it is harder."

Officer Dave Porras said Beyea, the grandson of a Los Angeles traffic officer, was quick to share action stories from his new job.

"He would tell me about the foot pursuits and the narcotics arrests and the fun he was having," a tearful Porras said to the overflow crowd at Praiswater Funeral Home in Van Nuys.

"Jim once told me that he couldn't believe he was actually paid to do police work. But you can't put a price on what happened this week. Jim was out there because he wanted to be out there."

Beyea was shot when he confronted a 16-year-old youth suspected of burglarizing an electronics store.

Authorities said Beyea's killer was Robert Jay Steele, a suspected gang member who was later cornered in the attic of a nearby house and shot to death by other officers when he attempted to reach for a gun. An accused accomplice in the burglary, Alberto B. Hernandez, 19, was captured and has been charged with murder and burglary.

The two teen-agers "were both active members" of a street gang that often gathers in East San Fernando

Valley parks, including Sun Valley Park, where Steele was also known as a talented member of a youth baseball team, Sgt. Ray Davies said.

Beyea was the first Los Angeles police officer to die in the line of duty in a year and the 175th killed since 1907.

PART TWO
THE KILLERS

KILLER ON THE RUN

WILDER CHARGED WITH SLAYING HOUSEWIFE

SOUTH FLORIDA SUN-SENTINEL
April 7, 1984

A S FEDERAL FUGITIVE Christopher Bernard Wilder continued to elude authorities Friday, he was charged with the first-degree murder of an Oklahoma City housewife and another grim stop-off was added to the trail FBI agents suspect he has taken west from South Florida since March.

The charge filed in Junction City, Kansas, near where the woman's body was found March 26 is the first murder charge lodged against the Boynton Beach man who authorities suspect has gone from Miami to Las Vegas, Nev., on a kidnapping and murdering spree.

Wilder, 39, has been charged in Florida for the kidnap and rape of a Tallahassee college coed. The electrical contractor, part-time race car driver and self-styled photographer was placed on the FBI's Ten Most Wanted Fugitives list this week and is now suspected in at least eight abductions or murders of young, attractive women.

In Miami, FBI agents Friday released a 1981 video recording of a well-groomed and quiet-spoken Wilder, sitting relaxed before a camera and discussing what he called his goals, his need to meet more women and his description of who the right person for him would be.

Agents said they hope broadcasts of the cassette tape across the nation will help lead to Wilder's capture.

"It's a hell of an investigative aid for us," said bureau spokesman Dennis Erich. "Anyone who has seen this and then sees him will know it's him."

The FBI declined to identify where the six-minute tape came from. In what appears to be an interview for a dating service, the cassette depicts Wilder in a yellow sports shirt and jeans, sitting on a couch while being questioned by an unseen interviewer.

"I have what I call a need to meet and socialize on a

more wider basis than I've been," Wilder said. "I want to date. I want to socially meet and enjoy the company of a number of women."

When asked what his objectives for the future were in the three-year-old tape, Wilder said, "Hopefully meeting the right person. Somebody with depth, somebody with some background specifically to themselves. Somebody that I can feel comfortable with."

Wilder discussed his contracting business, his hobbies of car racing and water skiing and his dislike for "bar-hopping" as a means of meeting women.

"Barhopping is not and never has been one of my greater joys," he said. "I've reached the point where I can't go to Big Daddy's and feel comfortable.

"I'm a little out of that category," he added with a laugh.

The version of a reserved and good-natured Wilder captured on the videocassette seems a contrast to the man authorities across the country suspect him to be.

Wilder, who investigators believe fled from his Palm Beach County home in mid-March following the disappearances of two Miami models, was charged Friday with the murder of Suzanne Wendy Logan, a 21-year-old Oklahoma City woman who disappeared March 25 from a shopping mall.

The victim's body was found the next day in a picnic area at Milford Lake in Geary County, Kans.

Wilder "very definitely is our man," said Geary County Deputy Sheriff William Deppish. The warrant listed bond for the elusive fugitive at $2 million.

Officials said Wilder became the prime suspect because Mrs. Logan's murder was similar to the other disappearances and the murder fits into the path and time frame of the fugitive's alleged trek west.

"We suspect Wilder because of the way he operates, tying a women's wrists with duct tape, bruises about the wrists and body and long knife wounds in the back," said John DiPersio, Geary County undersheriff.

"The time schedule and the geography make him a prime suspect," said Max Geiman, FBI special agent in Kansas City, Mo.

Positive identification of Mrs. Logan was made Thursday through dental records. A fisherman had discovered her body partially hidden beneath the low branches of a pine tree on the banks of Milford Lake near Junction City. An autopsy showed she had died of one stab wound to the back.

FBI officials in Washington this week said that if Wilder is responsible for the murders and disappearances he is sought for, then it would be a classic case of sexual serial murders. Wilder was placed on the Ten Most Wanted list faster than any other fugitive before.

Agents said Wilder approaches young women in shopping malls and identifies himself as a photographer. He comments on the woman's appearance and potential as a model, and then tries to persuade her to accompany him for a photo session.

In separate incidents since 1980 in Palm Beach County and Australia, Wilder has been charged with abducting and assaulting young women after presenting himself as a model photographer. He is wanted on a kidnapping warrant for the Australian case and for violation of probation in the local case.

The massive search for Wilder began in late March after FBI agents connected the kidnapping and rape of a Florida State University student with two earlier disappearances from the Miami area.

After fleeing his Boynton Beach home authorities believe he headed west and is suspected of leaving several disappearances and murders in his wake:

- Feb. 26; Rosario Gonzalez, 20, a part-time model, disappeared from the Miami Grand Prix. Still missing.

- March 3; Elizabeth Kenyon, 23, a part-time teacher and model, disappeared from Miami. Her car was found abandoned at the airport. Still missing.

- March 18; Theresa Ferguson, 21, an aspiring model, disappeared from a Merritt Island shopping mall. Her body was found three days later in an isolated creek near Haines City in Polk County.

- March 20; a 19-year-old Florida State University coed was abducted from a Tallahassee shopping mall after a man identified as Wilder offered her $25 an hour to pose for pictures. She escaped from a Bainbridge, Ga., motel where she told authorities Wilder had tortured and raped her. Wilder was charged with abduction.

- March 23; Terry Walden, 24, a nursing student, disappeared from Beaumont, Tex. Her body was found in a canal outside the city three days later.

- March 25; Suzanne Wendy Logan, 21, a housewife, disappeared from Oklahoma City, Okla. Her body was found in a picnic area at Milford Lake in Geary County, Kans., the next day.

- March 29; Sheryl Bonaventura, 18, vanished from a Grand Junction, Colo., shopping mall. Still missing.

- April 1; Michelle Korfman, 17, an aspiring model, disappeared from a Las Vegas, Nev., shopping mall after appearing in a fashion show. Still missing.

Sun-Sentinel staff writers contributed to this report.

WILDER LED DOUBLE LIFE IN SOUTH FLORIDA

April 15, 1984

Long before Christopher Bernard Wilder became the most wanted fugitive in America, he haunted the fringes of South Florida's modeling and fashion circles.

Investigators said Wilder was able to enter these circles through his cunning charm, smooth talk, money and most of all, his camera.

Armed with these credentials, Wilder bluffed his way into top beauty pageants and fashion shows and stalked shopping centers and beaches as a self-styled photographer and talent agent. At least one modeling agency sent him models for photo sessions.

"Wilder lurked in the shadows," said Ken Whittaker, Jr., a 28-year-old private detective who first brought Wilder's name to authorities. "He was cunning and smooth, very manipulative with women."

"He was active for quite a while," said Tom Neighbors, a Palm Beach County Sheriff's detective. "He had a nice scam he used to get close to the type of women he liked."

A massive search for Wilder across 8,000 miles of the country ended Friday when the Australian-born electrical contractor and race car driver accidentally shot himself to death while struggling with a police officer at a small town gas station in New Hampshire.

Wilder, whose journey was grimly charted by the abductions or murders of at least 11 women, appears to have led a double life: one opulent, marked by financial success, fast cars and attractive women; the other sinister, tainted by arrests, investigations and suspicions.

That is the assessment of court records and those who came to know the 39-year-old Wilder.

"As far as I knew he was a real photographer," said a woman who met Wilder through car racing and once went to his home for a photo session. She asked not to be identified.

"I'm flabbergasted by this whole thing," she said. "He must have been flipped out to be doing all these things and hiding so much. He seemed like a normal, nice guy."

The startling chain of events has had a greater impact on Wilder's family in Australia. His mother and American-born father have gone into seclusion while a 41-year-old brother Stephen has been in the United States aiding the FBI.

"The family has been completely broken up," said Valerie Wilder, a sister-in-law. "Life has not been easy. We are trying to live one day at a time."

She said Christopher Wilder first came to the United States when he was one year old. He spent much of the next several years on the road, as his father, who was in the U.S. Navy, was transferred about the nation. The Wilders did not permanently return to Australia until 1959. Christopher Wilder, the second oldest of four brothers, moved back to the United States when he was 25.

"Chris was always a perfect gentleman in the way he treated me," his shaken sister-in-law said. "My kids adored him."

But detectives said their investigations suggest Wilder's gentle and friendly demeanor shrouded a darker side.

"I felt he was a Jekyll and Hyde character from the beginning," said attorney and investigator Ken Whittaker, Sr., former special agent in charge of the FBI's Miami office.

Early last month, Whittaker and his son repeatedly questioned Wilder and began to suspect him in the disappearances of two Miami models. They had been hired by one of the models' family to find her.

A week later, Wilder checked his three dogs into a kennel and embarked on an odyssey that took him from Florida to California and then back across the nation to the tiny town of Colebrook, N.H., five minutes from the Canadian border.

FBI agents suspect the macabre trek included stop-offs in at least nine cities where women were abducted or murdered.

Wilder's neighbors on Mission Hill Road in Boynton Beach told of occasional parties, several female visitors and a racing Porsche parked atop a trailer. Lately, the car and property have been the focus of police detectives and newspaper reporters.

"It's become a historical monument," resident Ken Bankowski said of the Porsche.

Though investigators said the cross-country rampage of rape and killing has stopped with Wilder's death, many mysteries surrounding the man remain unanswered.

Joseph Corless, special agent in charge of the FBI office

in Miami, said the bureau will continue to investigate Wilder's past for possible links to other unsolved disappearances.

"We are not eliminating anything," said Detective Neighbors.

Some of Wilder's movements in recent years have already been documented.

Wilder was captured on film at the 1983 Miss Florida pageant in Fort Lauderdale. Pageant officials said last week that a review of videotape taken during an Oct. 1, 1982, media day at the beach shows Wilder among about a dozen photographers. The tape was turned over to the FBI.

Elizabeth Kenyon, 23, a part-time teacher and model who disappeared March 5 from Miami, was a finalist in that pageant and possibly met Wilder there. She is still missing and authorities said Wilder is a suspect in her disappearance.

"He was at the pageant and he represented himself as a photographer for *Pix* magazine from Australia," said Grant Gravitt, one of the pageant's producers.

Blaine Davis, media coordinator for the pageant, said Wilder presented a media identification card but it apparently was not checked with the Australian magazine for authenticity.

"Normally, with a magazine from Australia, I wouldn't check," Davis said. "He did present some credentials that were acceptable at the time."

In Australia, *Pix* officials said there is no record of the magazine ever employing Wilder or purchasing photographs from him.

More recently, in what the FBI termed a "close call," a 20-year-old Fort Lauderdale model was forced to turn down an invitation Feb. 23 to pose for Wilder when she couldn't arrange transportation to his Boynton Beach home.

The young woman, who talked on condition that her name not be used, said a photographer told her Wilder had seen photos of her, was "dying to meet her" and wanted to take her photograph for a beer advertisement at the then upcoming Miami Grand Prix.

"When Wilder called later that night, he said he was doing a Budweiser commercial and wanted to do a shoot in his garage, with a car he was going to race the next day," the model said. "I thought that was strange, taking pictures in a garage. But since my photographer recommended him, I didn't think any more about it."

The model said she decided against the trip when her parents, fearing something was "not right," refused to lend her their car.

"I called Wilder back and told him I couldn't make it," she said. "He seemed upset and wanted me to take a cab. But when I said no, he asked me to meet him the next day at the race. I told him I was busy."

Aspiring model Rosario Gonzalez disappeared from the Miami Grand Prix on Feb. 26. The 20-year-old woman is still missing. FBI agents said Wilder is a suspect in her disappearance.

"The FBI told me I was lucky," the Fort Lauderdale model said. "They said it was a close call. I'm still shook up about it."

Ted Martin, the photographer who attempted to set up the "shoot" between Wilder and the Fort Lauderdale woman, said he believed Wilder was a legitimate photographer. He had met Wilder at a fashion show at the Cutler Ridge Mall two years ago.

"I spent my time professionally with him," Martin said. "He was very into the business."

Investigators don't know how many other young aspiring models were unlucky enough to cross Wilder's path.

Detective Neighbors said he is suspected in a 1979 rape case. A 17-year-old girl reported at the time that she had been approached on the Lake Worth beach by a man claiming to be a talent agent for a prominent modeling agency in Fort Lauderdale. After luring the girl to his car, the man took her to a secluded area west of West Palm Beach and raped her. Neighbors said the woman recently told detectives her abductor was Wilder.

Investigators suspect Wilder used several aliases, business cards and ploys to lure young women to photo sessions where he would attempt to seduce them or rape them.

"There is evidence of different names and cards he would flash," said Neighbors. "That is part of his M.O. He had quite a line."

William Silvernail, who operates the Blackthorn modeling school in West Palm Beach, said Wilder approached his agency in 1981 as a freelance photographer looking for work. He didn't get any work, but Silvernail suspects Wilder may have taken a business card and then had copies made that identified him as a Blackthorn photographer.

Silvernail said his agency began getting calls from parents checking on a photographer who had approached their daughters. The name of the photographer was often different but the description was always the same: blond, balding and bearded — a description similar to Wilder.

At the Barbizon School of Modeling in Broward County, talent director Dorothy Girard said Wilder also used the name of her agency to approach young women and girls. In those cases, Mrs. Girard said Wilder was often wearing a Barbizon T-shirt.

"And, at that time, we didn't even have Barbizon T-shirts," she said. "When he was using our name, our students called up to check on him and we said, 'Forget it, he is not with us.'"

Some of the girls Wilder approached apparently didn't bother to check him out. He was arrested in 1980 for raping a 16-year-old girl after luring her from a West Palm Beach shopping mall with promises of appearing in a pizza advertisement as a Barbizon model.

According to court records, Wilder first told the girl to

strike poses for him at different stores in the mall. "My eyes are the camera," he told the girl, according to court records. "Don't pay attention to me."

Sheriff's Detective Arthur Newcomb, who arrested Wilder for the rape, later said in a court deposition that Wilder was believed to have continually used the photographer-agent ruse to seduce young women.

"[Wilder] stated this was a common operation, posing as this modeling agent, and that this is something he has done often," Newcomb said in a deposition. "He tries to get girls in order to have relations with them. I have non-crime reports that show this man has done this frequently. It is nothing he denies."

In that case, Wilder pleaded guilty to attempted sexual battery and was placed on five years' probation. He began receiving psychiatric counseling but never ended his life as self-styled fashion photographer.

Detectives said that in the early 1980s he built a studio in his home on Mission Hill Road. The room was complete with developing, printing and lighting equipment, backdrops and cosmetic supplies. A friend said Wilder even had fans "for blowing a model's hair back."

In December 1982, two months after he had bluffed his way into the Miss Florida Pageant, Wilder was arrested in Australia and charged with the abduction and indecent assault on two teen-agers he had lured from the beach with a promise of modeling jobs. Wilder had first taken the girls to a zoo where he took their pictures as they posed on a rock sculpture.

Police said there was no film in the camera he was using. On April 4, he failed to show for a court hearing on the case in Australia.

According to records in Australia and with Interpol, Wilder showed the girls a card identifying himself as a photographer for Tide International, a talent agency located on Worth Avenue in Palm Beach.

Detective Neighbors said Wilder was associated with Tide as a freelance photographer in the early '80s. According to the detective, models were referred to Wilder's home studio for photo sessions.

"He used [Tide] as a source for models," said Neighbors. "He would call and say I need a model and they would send one over. He legitimately hired them. What he did with the pictures, I don't know."

Neighbors said the sheriff's office has received no complaints from any Tide models that posed for Wilder. He said several that were interviewed said Wilder had acted very professionally and they expressed shock that he was suspected in several abductions or murders.

Tom Davis, owner of Tide, said Wilder was not associated with the business. While Davis acknowledged that he had met Wilder through Grand Prix racing, he said Wilder was not one of about 40 freelance photographers associated with Tide.

"We never sent him models, no way on that," said Davis.

Though Neighbors said Wilder may have had arrangements with other agencies throughout the area in the early '80s, he said Wilder removed the studio and photographic equipment from his home after his arrest in Australia. The self-styled fashion photographer then began dropping off his film at a local Kmart store to be developed.

Sun-Sentinel staff writers Ott Cefkin and Patricia Sullivan, along with correspondent Nick Yardley in Australia, contributed to this report.

WILDER VICTIMS STILL MISSING 1 YEAR LATER

February 23, 1985

Haydee Gonzalez will think about the wedding that was planned for her daughter last June and she will cry.

Delores Kenyon will talk about the bedroom, filled with her daughter's unused belongings, and she, too, has to cry.

It has been 12 months now since Rosario Gonzalez disappeared and nearly as long since Beth Kenyon has been gone, but to each of the missing young women's families, the pain and the questions have not been diminished by time.

Though it has been a year since Christopher Wilder began a cross-country odyssey of kidnap, rape and murder that authorities believe started with the disappearances of the two South Florida women and ended in his own death 8,000 miles later, he keeps a grim hold on many.

The families of Gonzalez and Kenyon still don't know the fate of their daughters. Neither do Wilder's many investigators. And they don't know how many other unknown victims he may have claimed, either.

With the suspected murderer gone, the families, FBI agents and police officers continue to follow clues and search for the missing women, all the while piecing together bits of the Wilder puzzle.

"It has been a year and we still cry," said Delores Kenyon, of Pompano Beach. Delores and William Kenyon's daughter, Beth, 23, was last seen March 6 with Wilder at a Coral Gables gas station.

"You can't help but cry," she said this week. "I don't think my heart could be broken any worse. We've gone through a year of this, and we are still at that gas station. We don't know what happened to her after that."

"Whatever has happened we will accept as God's way. But we need to know what happened," said Haydee Gonzalez, of Miami. Rosario Gonzalez, 20, daughter of Haydee and Blas Gonzalez, disappeared from the Miami Grand Prix a year ago this weekend.

In the last year, the two families have hired private

detectives, consulted psychics, distributed thousands of "missing" posters, placed newspaper ads from here to El Salvador and traveled as far as Mexico and Canada in hopes of finding their daughters — whether it would be to find them alive or not.

The Gonzalezes and two relatives were arrested for trespassing on Mother's Day last May when they searched the outside of Wilder's Boynton Beach home for clues. Mrs. Gonzalez said it was the frustration of not knowing; she had to do something. The charges were later dropped.

The families have found no trace of the two women. Of the 13 women Wilder is believed to have abducted, six were murdered, four escaped their abductor and three are still missing. The missing are Kenyon, Gonzalez and Colleen Orsborne, 15, who disappeared from Daytona Beach on March 15.

Wilder was killed April 13 while struggling for a gun with a state trooper in Colebrook, N.H.

Not knowing what happened to the missing women is the thing that hurts their families most; it hurts more than knowing.

"They have found their daughters and buried them," Delores Kenyon said of some of the other families from which Wilder took a daughter. "We don't even know what happened to ours."

"The not knowing is the worst thing about this," said Haydee Gonzalez.

That's why the Gonzalez family had gone as far as Mexico City looking for Rosario; why each weekend they take a drive out to a different spot of western Dade County to look for her in the Everglades areas; and why they will be at the Miami Grand Prix this weekend distributing 10,000 flyers with her photograph on them.

And that's why the Kenyons call the FBI week in and week out to see what is happening on their daughter's case; why they have spent thousands of dollars on three different private detective agencies; and why they have followed even a psychic's advice and searched underbrush as far away as Alabama for their daughter.

And that's also why the FBI and police, even close to a year after Wilder's death, follow any plausible lead or clue in an effort to locate the missing women.

"It is a continuing process," said Miami Police Detective Harvey Wasserman. "Leads still come in. We still follow them. But so far nothing has worked out."

"We follow up on any kind of lead that comes in," said FBI spokesman Joe Del Campo. "We won't stop until all logical investigation has been completed and all leads are followed out."

As late as last week, Miami police got a call that Rosario Gonzalez had been seen in Washington, D.C. The tip didn't check out.

And for the FBI, following the leads has recently led agents to the death row of a California prison to talk to a man who once knew Wilder and is now awaiting execution for murder, a source with knowledge of the investigation said.

The source said the prisoner claimed he could help investigators find the missing women, but information he provided did not check out. Del Campo acknowledged that agents went to California recently, but would not confirm that they spoke to a prison inmate.

While continuing a search for the missing women, the FBI is also pursuing another branch of investigation. Agents are following Wilder back in time along a trail of credit-card, telephone and other traceable records.

Del Campo said agents intend to trace Wilder's trail backward for years and will compare each stop to any unsolved crimes in that area that involve the abduction, rape or murder of young, attractive women.

"It is very much an ongoing investigation. We are piecing together the Wilder puzzle," Del Campo said. "In the case of Mr. Wilder, there could be victims from years in the past that we don't know about yet. We will leave no stone unturned."

Wilder had a record of arrests for sexual offenses dating back to the 1970s in Palm Beach County and his native Australia. So far, investigators have learned that Wilder crossed the country in the year before the murderous spree that made him the most wanted fugitive in America. Agents said they have attributed a 1983 kidnapping and rape of a young woman in San Mateo, Calif., to Wilder.

"It is difficult to track," Del Campo said. "We are trying to put it all together. It is going to take time."

Time is something the families of Rosario Gonzalez and Beth Kenyon have had to pass in agonizing pain since their daughters were reported missing last year.

Gonzalez was last seen Feb. 26, 1984, distributing samples of an aspirin product at the Miami Grand Prix. Investigators have placed the aspiring model at the race that day speaking at one point to a man fitting Wilder's description.

Wilder, an electrical contractor with an affinity for car racing and photography, had raced his black Porsche in a preliminary Grand Prix race a day earlier and had returned to the race grounds Feb. 26 with his camera, the device investigators say he used often to lure women to their deaths.

The missing woman's family hopes the 10,000 flyers they will distribute this weekend will bring out new information on her disappearance. The flyers offer a $50,000 reward for information leading to her whereabouts.

"The FBI has not proven it was Wilder who took her," Mrs. Gonzalez said. "There were people from all over the country at the Grand Prix. There were yachts from all over. Maybe some of these people will be back this year and will see her picture and remember something that will help us."

In her heart, Gonzalez believes that her daughter,

who had planned to get married last June, can be found alive.

"I feel she is still alive," she said. "I have no idea where, but it could be she was kidnapped and taken away somewhere."

The Gonzalezes and Kenyons share a unique, though tragic, bond. Family members often call each other to console one another and share information on their similar searches. When the Kenyons were pursuing a tip that their daughter might be in El Salvador, members of the Gonzalez family came to Pompano Beach from Miami to translate telephone calls.

"We share what we know and stay in contact, usually every few weeks," said Selva Menendez, a cousin of the Gonzalez family who often acts as a translator for Haydee and Blas Gonzalez, who speak little English. "We believe if we find one of the girls, the other will be nearby."

The trail of Beth Kenyon, also an aspiring model like many of Wilder's victims, ended at the gas station near the Coral Gables elementary school where she taught. Her car was found at Miami International Airport. Her family has never stopped looking for her.

"If somebody calls up and says our daughter is on the moon, we will send somebody to the moon to look for her," said Mrs. Kenyon.

But the family's search has come up painfully short of information on what happened to Beth. The posters mailed to churches and sheriffs' offices and supermarkets across Florida have resulted in no plausible leads. A six-day search for a cabin in North Alabama where a psychic said the woman might be also proved fruitless. Dead ends — just as with leads to Canada and South America.

"We are still where we were March 6. We haven't gotten her past that gas station," Delores Kenyon said.

Like Haydee Gonzalez, Mrs. Kenyon keeps a small hope in her heart that her daughter is still alive. She has shipped all of Beth's belongings from her Coral Gables apartment to the family's permanent home in Lockport, N.Y. And she waits, hopes and prays for the day her daughter will use them again.

"Everything is waiting for her," Mrs. Kenyon said. "Her bedroom is waiting for her. Everything is as it was. You just have to hope, that's all. And pray."

And then she began to cry.

DARK DISGUISE

KILLING OF SPOUSE PUTS AN END TO MAN'S DOUBLE LIFE

Crime: A former Granada Hills resident is in jail in Florida on a murder charge. Wife says he claimed to work for the CIA and married again without divorcing her.

LOS ANGELES TIMES
September 29, 1991

IN HIS GRANADA HILLS office, David Russell Miller surrounded himself with reminders of the things that meant the most to him.

A fixture at civic and business functions across the San Fernando Valley, the former Chamber of Commerce president covered a wall in his office with the photos of the important people he knew and had met. There was the governor, local assemblymen, international figures such as Oliver North, even Desmond Tutu.

But there was no photo of his wife, Dorothy. None of her two young children. Indeed, most of the people who knew Miller — including those who worked with him for years — say they did not know he was even married.

Neither did saleswoman Jayne Marie Maghy when she met him on a plane in January. And after a six-week romance that included limousine rides and meals at expensive restaurants, she married him in Las Vegas. But soon after the glow of her whirlwind courtship dimmed, the new Mrs. Miller became suspicious of her husband's business and personal dealings.

With the help of a private detective she stumbled onto the other Mrs. Miller and on Sept. 15 confronted her husband.

It was a confrontation that cost her her life, police say. Jayne Miller was shot to death in the Central Florida town where the couple had moved earlier this year. David Miller, 41, is being held in a Sanford, Fla., jail without bail on a charge of murder.

The killing has sent a wave of astonishment across the Valley and served to pull back the veil that shielded David Miller's secret life.

Many who thought they knew him now count themselves as victims of a con man. Some wonder if the violent end to David Miller's double life could have been averted if they had voiced suspicions they had early on.

Dorothy Miller said she met David Miller in Granada Hills in 1979. The recently divorced owner of a hair salon was raising two young boys and after she met Miller in an attorney's office, a romance began.

Dorothy Miller said her future husband told her that he had been divorced once and had just moved to the Valley from the Washington area where he had held government jobs, including being an aide in the Nixon Administration. He was raised in Sardis, Ohio, and wore an Ohio University ring. University officials last week confirmed that he attended the school but refused to reveal other information until Miller cleared up financial obligations to the school.

Within six months, the couple moved in together and later bought a house on Aldea Avenue in Granada Hills. They weren't formally married until Aug. 11, 1985, when they drove to Las Vegas and were wed in a roadside chapel. Dorothy Miller still has the marriage license. She says there was never any divorce.

As a Valley-based lobbyist, David Miller initially specialized in representing the printing industry on state legislative issues. In 1987, his reputation as a lobbyist landed him a job as a legislative aide to Assemblyman Tom McClintock (R-Thousand Oaks), but McClintock said he fired Miller after six months because of unexplained absences and poor performance. Miller then opened an office called David Miller & Associates in the same building that housed the Granada Hills Chamber of Commerce.

His firm expanded to include developers as clients, and civic activities had him involved in chamber functions. He served a term as president of the chamber and then as president of the United Chambers of Commerce, an umbrella organization for 20 Valley chambers.

Those who know Miller described him as a name-dropper who drove a Jaguar and stayed at first-class hotels while traveling. He took clients and business acquaintances out for pricey meals and picked up the tabs. Some said Miller told them he was an attorney, though there is no record of him as a member of the California Bar.

"He was so good at stories," said a businesswoman who knew Miller for years but who didn't want to be identified. "They would get long and complicated. He could tell wonderful stories, but there was always the feeling that that's what they were, stories."

It was unclear why Miller kept his wife away from his business and social interests. Dorothy Miller said that the story her husband told her was that the life he led in California was a front.

His real work, he said, was for the CIA.

"From the day I met him, he always told me CIA stories," she said in a recent interview from Belle Vernon, Pa., where she now lives. "He told me it was freelance work. He was always involved in international incidents. Whatever was in the news."

Though admittedly embarrassed now, Dorothy Miller said she believed her husband. And there was some evidence that he was traveling abroad. He often brought back souvenirs from foreign countries and there were calls home that were put through by Spanish-speaking operators.

Sometimes, he told her of international events that she saw on the news. Sometimes, he told her of events that never hit the news — like the time he came home with a cut leg and said he had been grazed by a bullet.

"It was convincing," she said. "He could explain enough and include enough details to make it believable. When I had questions he just told me I would have to trust him on it. He told me that a lot."

Dorothy Miller said she met few of the people her husband did business with in the Valley and never once set foot in the office because her husband said it would be a security risk. He explained that the business was a CIA front set up to trap a target in a web of unspecified international crime.

But the trap was apparently never sprung. In 1989, David Miller moved his wife and her two sons to

Orlando, Fla. She said he explained that he was closing the California office and selling their house because the family could be in danger.

"He said it was for security reasons," Dorothy Miller said. "He said, 'You have to trust me.'"

The Millers bought a new house in Orlando and Dorothy got a job at a local hair salon. She said her husband continued to travel, coming home for only a few days at a time and always regaling her with tales of international intrigue.

What Dorothy Miller did not know was that her husband did not close his Granada Hills office and continued to live in the home they had shared there. And while it is unknown where all of his travels took him, it is clear his business and civic activities in the Valley continued until at least early this year.

Business acquaintances said that until early this year Miller was heavily involved in establishing the San Fernando Valley Leadership Program, a 10-month seminar in which citizen activists and business and government officials spend one day a month learning about and discussing an issue of public importance, such as environmental health, transportation or crime.

Participants in the program, sometimes numbering as many as 30, each paid $700 tuition when it was first instituted by Miller in 1987. The program, deemed a success by alumni such as Richard Alarcon, now Valley deputy for Mayor Tom Bradley, has been repeated every year since and the tuition has risen to $1,200. Inspired by its success, Miller & Associates began efforts to market the concept in other communities across the country.

Heavily involved in the program and also anticipating an increase in his company's lobbying and business consulting clients, Miller added Ross B. Hopkins, a former public affairs manager for Lockheed Corp., to his firm in November.

But the anticipated boom went bust, Hopkins said.

"He overextended," Hopkins said in an interview. "He counted on some contracts coming in that didn't come in."

Meantime, older sources of revenue — developments on which Miller had consulted — dried up as the work was finished and the contracts completed, Hopkins said. By early 1991, Miller was facing severe financial problems.

One creditor was Jacklyn Smith, owner of a Glendora firm that sells supplies to printing companies. Smith said she had given Miller, whom she had known for several years, a $17,000 loan that he repaid in January with a check that bounced. He then supplied another check from another bank, which also bounced, she said.

Smith later made a complaint to Los Angeles police, and investigators are attempting to determine if Miller committed fraud by giving her the checks knowing that they would not be covered by his banks.

Marge Russo, owner of a Reseda real-estate agency, said that she loaned Miller $6,500 for the purchase of a

Palm Springs condominium, but that he also failed to pay her back. She has since filed a lien against him.

According to records with the county recorder's office, Miller stopped making mortgage payments on his home and foreclosure proceedings had begun. Records also show his company failed to make at least $4,500 in tax payments to the state.

There were other debts as well. Hopkins said Miller stopped paying him and other employees soon after the start of the year. He said that on at least two occasions people came into the office looking for Miller and saying he owed them money.

But after the first of the year, Miller was rarely in the office to greet clients or creditors. While his financial world was crumbling, his personal life was apparently quite active.

Dorothy Miller said her husband spent the Christmas holidays in Orlando with her, but on Jan. 1 said he had to leave on a secret government assignment to South America.

But acquaintances said Miller actually flew back to his life in California. And while on the plane he met 33-year-old Jayne Maghy, a divorced mother, with whom a romance blossomed as soon as the plane touched down in Los Angeles.

According to Jodie Bowen, who describes herself as Maghy's best friend of 10 years, Miller "wined and dined" Maghy, boasting that he was an attorney worth $4 million.

There were front-row seats to *The Phantom of the Opera*, weekends at expensive bed-and-breakfast inns in Newport Beach, dinners at formal political functions.

"He was Prince Charming," Bowen said. "We had to go out and buy gowns for her so she could go to some of these functions with him. And he was obsessed with her. He called her every day. She was not happy with her job and thought, 'Here is someone who can take me away from this life.'"

Miller and Maghy were married Feb. 16 in a Las Vegas chapel. Bowen was the witness and that weekend the new Mrs. Miller won $3,000 playing video poker, a lucky start to what would be an ill-fated marriage.

David Miller did not keep the marriage a secret. Before the wedding, he had announced the marriage plans at a Granada Hills Chamber of Commerce dinner and after taking the vows he promptly called his associates from Las Vegas.

"It had been difficult getting a hold of him," Hopkins, his former associate, said of the period. "He was not in the office and I thought he was out trying to round up clients. Then he called and said, 'Guess what? We're married.'"

A group of friends and associates gathered at Miller's office on March 1 for a small reception for the couple. Hopkins said the happiness exhibited for the Millers was tinged with somberness. Some of those toasting Miller had not been paid by him in a month.

"I felt very bad for the staff because they were having problems and here the guy was getting married," Hopkins said.

At least one of Miller's friends believes that some people who knew him were uneasy about his marriage because his financial problems were becoming known. There were also rumors that he was already married.

"The joke was that he wanted to marry her quick, before she found out the truth about him," said a woman who worked with Miller on Chamber of Commerce projects. "Everybody knew he didn't have any money. And I think some people specifically knew he was already married."

After the marriage, Miller's financial problems quickly escalated, according to financial records and acquaintances. Business associates and creditors said it was increasingly difficult to contact Miller and recalled that in the instances where he was seen, he often became emotionally upset. Miller alternately explained that he was facing financial crisis or said he had cancer.

Alarcon, Mayor Bradley's Valley deputy, said that at a meeting of representatives of Valley political officeholders Miller tearfully announced that the Leadership Program would be his legacy in the Valley.

"When I asked him what was wrong, he told me he had cancer," Alarcon said.

John Dyer, a business consultant who subcontracted with Miller to share office space with him, said that on the occasions that Miller did come to the office, his moods changed noticeably.

"I think it was obvious to everyone who saw him that his state of mind had changed — changed considerably," Dyer said. "He would have times of anger — open outbursts. And sometimes, he was open, his friendly old self."

Miller was finally forced to close his office April 18, Hopkins said. Faced with foreclosure and liens for unpaid debts, he and his new wife signed ownership of the Granada Hills house over to a bail bondsman named Bert Hopper on May 7, according to county records.

The mortgage foreclosure was withdrawn, but other debt holders said they never got their money. Hopper did not return repeated phone calls for comment on the house transfer.

Miller then moved his new wife to Sanford, Fla., a small town outside Orlando. Dorothy Miller said that by this time her husband had already moved her from Orlando to Belle Vernon, Pa., once again telling her that the move was required as a security precaution.

But after making the move, Dorothy Miller said her husband stopped his routine of calling her every day. He also stopped making even infrequent visits home and she had no idea where he was. She said years of building suspicion finally got to her and she began making calls.

First, she said, the CIA told her David Miller was not an employee, freelance or otherwise. Next, calls to Chamber of Commerce officials in the Valley revealed that her husband had been active in the area until only a few months earlier — until he had gotten married.

"I thought, 'That's funny, since I already am his wife,'" Dorothy Miller said. "But nobody knew about me there. They thought I was a crazy woman."

Dorothy Miller said that when her husband did finally telephone her in midsummer, she confronted him and he admitted that he had remarried. She said she cut off all communication with him and asked the police in Belle Vernon to investigate.

Meantime, David Miller had taken his new wife and her parents to Europe in June despite his financial burdens. It is unclear how he paid for the trip. Vince Bertolini, also a former United Chambers of Commerce president who had worked with Miller, said he happened to run into his old friend June 26 in the lobby of a hotel in Rome.

"It was very strange," Bertolini said. "He told me he was representing the Kuwaiti government, resolving issues from the Persian Gulf War. It was kind of off the wall."

Bertolini said Miller also acknowledged that he was having financial difficulties and said the experience taught him that "you really know who your friends are."

After returning from Europe, the marriage of David and Jayne Miller foundered. Police said the two separated after repeated fights and each sought restraining orders against the other. Jayne Miller said in court documents that her husband had repeatedly threatened to kill her.

Suspicious of her husband's dealings and debts, Jayne Miller next hired private detective Bob Brown to make inquiries. Brown said Jayne Miller told him her husband had claimed to be a tax attorney in California who moved to Florida to work at Disney World.

Brown made routine computer checks and found David Miller's name linked with the name Dorothy Miller on car and house titles and tax rolls. He found no record of the couple being divorced.

"I told Jayne that it looked like this guy already had a wife," Brown said. "It looks like he had two houses, one here and one in California. He had evidently been commuting back and forth between wives."

Using Brown's information and old phone records left behind by her husband, Jayne Miller tracked down Dorothy Miller in Pennsylvania and the two confirmed each other's existence. Dorothy Miller said Jayne Miller told her that she was determined to confront their shared husband and expose him by going to the media with the story of the high-profile bigamist.

"I told her he was dangerous and warned her to stay away from him," Dorothy Miller said.

Brown said he gave his client the same warning. And her friend Bowen sent her a plane ticket so that she could move back to California.

But Jayne Miller would never take the flight. On

Sept. 15, according to Sanford police records, Jayne Miller called her husband and told him she was removing his property from a self-storage locker and that he would have to come and pick it up.

Brown believes his client planned to empty her husband's property out of the locker and then leave before he arrived. She may also have felt less fear of her husband because a month earlier she had insisted that he turn a handgun he owned over to police for safekeeping and he had agreed to do so.

However, Jayne Miller was still at the storage facility when her husband arrived. According to police, the couple began arguing about Miller's other wife and he struck Jayne Miller in the face. When she walked to her car, saying she was going to call the police, David Miller calmly walked back to his car and got a handgun, police said.

Miller walked up to his wife's car and fired six times through the driver's side window at her, police said. He then walked around to the other side of the car and fired once more into the car, police said. Two cabdrivers who had been called by David Miller to help him take away his belongings said they witnessed the shooting and tried to aid Jayne Miller, but she was dead. They also held her husband and the gun until police arrived.

Sanford Police Chief Steven Harriett said the gun Miller used to kill his wife was the weapon he had checked in at the police station Aug. 27 for safekeeping.

However, Miller had reclaimed the weapon three days later. Harriett said the department had no authority to keep the gun from him. "We had no basis to know what he was going to do with it," the police chief said.

Brown said he doubted his client knew her husband had retrieved the gun before going to the storage locker.

"She would never have gone there if she knew he had the gun back," he said. "She made a mistake and paid for it."

Harriett said that while his investigators are aware of the accusations of bigamy and fraud surrounding Miller, they are not actively investigating the suspect's activities before the killing. "It's interesting and intriguing, but not pertinent to our case," he said.

Some who knew Miller believe that more will remain unknown about him than what is known.

"It's so frustrating," said Dorothy Miller, who is now living on welfare. "David did a lot of things nobody can explain or that they thought he would never have been able to do. . . . He's a bad person and what he did wasn't right."

There is also at least some frustration and guilt in the Valley. The woman who worked with David Miller on Chamber of Commerce functions said she believes that there are many who knew him who now wish they had voiced suspicions about his previous marriage and financial problems.

"I firmly believe that all of us knew it, but nobody

wanted to take responsibility," she said. "No one wants to be connected with it now. They just say he was a nice guy and they are shocked. Nobody wants to open up and say we should have told poor Jayne."

NOTE: A Florida jury later rejected David Russell Miller's insanity defense and found him guilty of murdering his wife. He was sentenced to life in prison.

THE STALKER

MAN CHARGED IN 1982 DEATH
ALLEGES POLICE VENDETTA

LOS ANGELES TIMES
February 25, 1991

Jonathan Karl Lundh says he feels like a character in a suspense novel — an innocent man accused
of a heinous crime and left to use his own wits to clear
himself.

"It's like a cheap dime-store novel — I can't believe
what they are doing to me," Lundh said from behind the
bars of Los Angeles County Jail.

The 39-year-old Minnesota man pleaded not guilty last week to a charge he strangled a Cal State Northridge staff member nine years ago. Charges of robbery and rape in the case were dismissed because the statute of limitations for those crimes had expired.

Lundh appears bright and educated and can seemingly quote case law like an attorney. In fact, he has chosen to defend himself against the charges, although he said he quit Harvard Law School before getting a degree. He is soft-spoken and reserved. He has a young wife and friends who share his astonishment and outrage at the murder charge against him.

But authorities say it is the picture of Lundh as an innocent victim of the justice system that is fiction. They contend that he is a skilled con artist and killer who fabricates much of what he says about his life and hides the rest.

"There is no doubt that he is very bright," Los Angeles Police Detective Larry Bird said. "But I don't know whether I would believe anything he said. . . . He is a con man."

Police and prosecutors said that beneath Lundh's calm, articulate demeanor is a dangerous man who stalked women. It is a characterization that Lundh, who is being held without bail, said he finds as aggravating as his loss of freedom.

"I am not some mad dog cruising the streets, looking to prey on women," he said during a recent interview.

"Anybody who would do that to a woman should be put away.

"But it's not me. I am innocent!"

Lundh is accused of murdering Patty Lynne Cohen on April 27, 1982, in a case that received wide attention in Los Angeles.

Cohen, 40, an assistant to the dean of CSUN's School of Arts, was abducted from the garage of a Holiday Inn in Burbank, where she had attended a self-improvement seminar. Her nude body was found in the trunk of her car in a North Hollywood alley five days later.

Lundh, who according to court records has nine aliases and records of arrests for nonviolent crimes in at least five states, became a suspect less than two weeks after the slaying. He was later convicted of assaulting another woman outside the hotel just minutes before Cohen disappeared.

But he was never charged with the Cohen murder until last year — after police reopened the dormant investigation and said they found new evidence linking him to the case.

By then, Lundh had moved back to his native St. Paul. He was extradited to Los Angeles last month from a Minnesota prison where he was serving a sentence for grand theft in a case in which he used several thousand dollars of an unsuspecting woman's money to buy a car, authorities said.

In interviews and court records, Lundh has given different accounts of his background.

In 1983, according to records, he told a probation officer that he had attended Harvard Law School for a year before dropping out for financial reasons. He said he also attended six other universities, including Princeton.

Lundh told the probation officer that he made his living providing cars for film sets but also was an agent for several top entertainers. The officer concluded: "This defendant is viewed as a very sophisticated manipulator and con artist who uses his intelligence to defraud the public."

In a recent interview, Lundh added a year to his law school experience but said he left Harvard after two years because he was recruited to play defensive end with the Los Angeles Express, a now defunct professional football team.

"I wanted to attend law school but once I got there, my interests changed," he said.

Lundh said he was recruited by Express coaches because he had played defensive end for UCLA, from which he said he graduated in 1974. In addition to UCLA, Lundh said, "I did some time at the University of Hawaii."

But efforts to verify Lundh's claims were unsuccessful.

"We have no record of that person ever registering or attending the law school," Harvard spokeswoman Mary Ann Spartichino said.

Officials at UCLA and Hawaii also said they could not find any records indicating that Lundh attended those schools.

A media guide listing former UCLA football players did not include Lundh's name. And the Express lasted only a few seasons after beginning in 1982, a period during which Lundh spent most of his time in jails and prison.

When told that any discrepancies in the biography he furnished might be published, Lundh said his background was not important. "If you want to look for inconsistencies, look at the evidence in my case," he said.

Lundh said he is the victim of a police vendetta, that he was wrongly convicted of the 1982 assault at the Burbank hotel and is now a scapegoat for an unsuccessful investigation into Cohen's slaying.

"Why they singled me out, I don't know," Lundh said. "I was not in Burbank that evening and they know that. If there was a shred of evidence against me, they would have charged me in 1982, but they had the wrong man. It's not that they had insufficient evidence; they had no evidence.

"This has continued to disrupt my life for nine years," he added. "I've had my fill of justice."

But Bird, an investigator on the case since its start, said the evidence against Lundh has always been substantial. He said it was only with the reopening of the case and the gathering of additional evidence that prosecutors decided to file charges.

"It was a strong case," he said. "It's much stronger now."

Bird and the Los Angeles County prosecutor assigned to the case, Deputy Dist. Atty. Phillip H. Rabichow, have refused to disclose what additional evidence against Lundh was found.

But Lundh, who has access to legal documents on his case because he has acted as his own attorney, said an extradition warrant he studied stated that investigators had a witness who positively identified Lundh as a man seen driving Cohen's Mustang the night of her death.

Lundh scoffs at such evidence, saying it will be unbelievable to a jury hearing the witness nine years after the slaying.

"There is no possibility that someone is going to believe that somebody can remember something like that nine years later," he said.

According to police and court records, this is what happened April 27, 1982:

Cohen had gone to the Holiday Inn to attend a self-help seminar with about 100 others. When the meeting ended about 10:30 p.m., Ruth Kilday, another woman who had attended, saw a man standing in the hallway outside the seminar room. She said the man followed her to the parking lot, where he approached her with a knife as she was opening her car door.

Kilday was able to jump in the car and begin honking its horn to signal that she needed help. The man ran and she started her car and attempted to follow. But the man ran into the hotel's underground parking garage and Kilday gave up the pursuit.

Authorities said Cohen had parked in the garage and they believe that when she returned to her car, she encountered the man who ran from Kilday.

"I think he stalked her like he stalked the other victim," Rabichow said.

Cohen was reported missing the next day. Her car, with her body in the trunk, was not found until a North Hollywood resident saw it in an alley and recognized it from media reports about the woman's disappearance. Meanwhile, police had issued a drawing of the suspect made with the help of Kilday.

A week later, Lundh was arrested in North Hollywood when a police officer saw him in a stolen Corvette. Lundh gave the name John Robert Baker, and he immediately became a suspect in the Cohen and Kilday cases because of his likeness to the drawing of the suspect.

Although Police Chief Daryl F. Gates labeled Baker/ Lundh "a very likely suspect" at the time, prosecutors charged Lundh only with the auto theft and the assault on Kilday because there was insufficient evidence linking him to Cohen.

After his arrest, Lundh claimed that he was at a West Los Angeles gas station at 11 p.m. the night of the attack on Kilday, making it impossible for him to have been in Burbank. But during a 1983 trial, he was identified by

Kilday as her attacker and convicted of assault with a deadly weapon and auto theft. He was sentenced to four years in prison and released in 1986.

The Cohen murder case languished until a chance occurrence in 1990. A detective working on another murder case ran a routine check on the department's HITMAN — for Homicide Information Tracking Management Automation Network — computer looking for similar slayings.

Bird said the computer, which contains information on all Los Angeles homicides in the last decade, printed out the Cohen case in reply. Prosecutors then discussed the Cohen case with Bird but decided that it was not related to the case the other detective was investigating.

However, after reviewing the Cohen case, the prosecutors told Bird that there was nearly enough evidence to file charges against Lundh and urged that the case be reopened and the investigative ground covered again.

Bird said he located Lundh in St. Paul, where he had recently been paroled from prison for grand theft. Bird said he interviewed Lundh there, then returned to Los Angeles and began gathering new evidence.

In early 1990, Lundh was arrested in Colorado for violating his parole by leaving Minnesota and was returned to prison. Lundh said he left the state to get married and go on a honeymoon. Police believe that he left because he knew that the Cohen case had been reopened.

He was charged May 31, 1990, with Cohen's murder

and returned to Los Angeles in January. The trip back took a week because detectives had to drive him after he cited a fear of flying and refused to go on a plane.

He now awaits arraignment but that may be delayed because Lundh said he has not had enough time to prepare for the hearing.

Lundh's wife, Gale, who has moved to Los Angeles, is convinced her husband of 1½ years is not a con man or a killer.

"They have the wrong man," she said. "But in this system, it's not really innocent until proven guilty. It's guilty until proven innocent. The sad part is that the person who really did this is still out there."

NOTE: Lundh was tried twice for the murder of Patty Lynne Cohen. He represented himself in both trials. After the first trial ended with a deadlocked jury, he was tried again and found guilty of first-degree murder. He was sentenced to life in prison without the possibility of parole.

AMERICA'S
MOST WANTED

TARZANA MAN HELD IN MURDER
OF HIS MISSING FATHER

LOS ANGELES TIMES
December 4, 1987

A 21-YEAR-OLD Tarzana man was arrested Thursday on suspicion of murdering his father, a wealthy Japanese businessman who has been missing for seven months, Los Angeles police said.

Toru Sakai was being held without bail in the North Hollywood Division jail, Lt. Dan Cooke said.

Sakai's father, Takashi (Glenn) Sakai, 54, has not been seen since the day before he was reported missing April 21.

"Based on evidence we have obtained, we believe he was killed," Cooke said.

Police declined to disclose what evidence either indicates that the man is dead or links his son to the killing.

Toru Sakai was arrested when police officers conducted a search of family financial records at the Braewood Drive home he shares with his mother, Sanae Sakai.

Police said the suspect's parents had been estranged for about three years. The couple were in a legal battle over their finances and impending divorce at the time Takashi Sakai disappeared.

Sanae Sakai, 50, who operates a real-estate business out of the hillside home, was also arrested during the 7:15 a.m. search, but "during the all-day investigation, the investigators felt she should be released," Cooke said. He refused to elaborate.

Police said Takashi Sakai, founder of the Pacific Partners investment firm in Beverly Hills and a consultant to many other investment firms, was last seen leaving his office April 20.

Police declined to say where he was living at the time. He was reported missing the next day by a girlfriend.

Three days later, his car was found at Los Angeles International Airport, but authorities found no record of his having taken a flight.

Cooke said detectives then began gathering evidence of foul play.

Robert Brasch, president of World Trade Bank, of which Pacific Partners is a subsidiary, said Thursday that Takashi Sakai was a well-respected businessman and entrepreneur who had been involved in helping Japanese companies invest in businesses in the United States.

NOTE: After three days in jail Toru Sakai was released from jail when police and prosecutors determined they did not have enough evidence at that point to hold him on a murder charge. He then disappeared.

SAKAI FOUGHT KILLERS

May 24, 1988

Toru Sakai planned the murder of his father for three months, but from the moment the victim was lured inside a Beverly Hills mansion, things started going wrong, a man who said he helped Sakai with the killing testified Monday in Los Angeles Superior Court.

Takashi (Glenn) Sakai, 54, a wealthy international businessman who lived in Tarzana, was killed inside the home but not before a bloody and unexpected fight in which he almost was able to escape, Gregory Meier testified.

"I was behind the door," Meier said. "He took a couple of steps in, and I came up behind him. I was successful in hitting him in the neck, but he didn't go down. For some reason I thought I would be able to knock him out — like in the movies. But it doesn't work that way. He ran for the door.

"I helped Toru bring him back inside," Meier said. "We kept trying to knock him out."

It was only after the elder Sakai had been struck repeatedly with a steel bar and handcuffed that his son stabbed him to death in the house's basement, Meier testified.

Meier, 21, a friend of Toru Sakai's since they were members of the same high school tennis team, has been granted immunity in the case.

Sakai, also 21, has been charged with murder but is still being sought by authorities. His mother, Sanae Sakai, 51, has been charged with being an accessory to murder after the fact.

Meier revealed the details of the April 20, 1987, slaying during a preliminary hearing on the charge against Sanae Sakai. After Meier and other witnesses testified, she was ordered by Judge David M. Horwitz to stand trial in the case.

The body of Takashi Sakai, founder of Pacific Partners, an affiliate of the World Trade Bank in Beverly Hills, was found buried in Malibu Canyon in early February, about 10 months after his slaying.

According to Meier and authorities, Toru Sakai carried out the killing because his parents were embroiled in a bitter divorce and he feared that he and his mother, with whom he lived in the family's Tarzana home, would face financial difficulties.

"He told me, basically, that he hated his father and he didn't know what else to do," Meier said.

Discussed the Slaying

Meier said that on three occasions in early 1987 he and Toru Sakai discussed the killing. But Meier said he wanted no part of the plan. Meier said he finally agreed to help his friend in early April 1987, when Toru said he had paid another friend $1,000 to do the job but the friend failed to follow through.

"I didn't volunteer," Meier said. "He persuaded me. He told me he would help me out when I needed him."

Meier said the plan was to lure Takashi Sakai to the empty Beverly Hills home at 718 Crescent Drive that Sanae Sakai was managing for a Japanese investor. Once there, Sakai would be kidnapped and taken to Malibu Canyon and then killed and buried, he testified.

In early April, the two friends dug a grave in a secluded spot off Malibu Canyon Road, Meier testified. Then on April 20, Meier said he went to the Beverly Hills home and waited while Toru met his father at a nearby hotel to ask the elder Sakai to come with him to the home.

When he arrived at the house, Takashi Sakai was attacked, subdued after a struggle at the front door and then thrown down the basement stairs, Meier said.

"He was moaning and yelling for help at the bottom of the stairs," Meier said.

Change in Plan

After that, Toru Sakai decided to change the plan and carry out the killing in the basement, Meier said.

"He brought out a knife and asked me to go down and finish off his father," Meier said.

Meier said he refused and then watched Toru take the knife down to the basement. When Meier later went down, he saw the older Sakai had been stabbed to death. He said the body was then wrapped in trash bags, rolled in the blood-soaked rug from the house's entrance hall and loaded into Toru's Porsche. The two then took the body to Malibu Canyon for burial, Meier said.

Meier said he and Toru spent the next two days getting rid of evidence. He said they dropped Takashi Sakai's car at Los Angeles International Airport, took the murder weapon and the piece of carpet from the entrance hall of the Beverly Hills house to a landfill in Glendale and painted over blood-spattered walls in the house.

"We put several coats in the basement," he said.

Meier testified that he later received $1,400 from Toru Sakai for his part in the killing.

A carpet salesman and an installer also testified Monday that two days after the killing, Sanae Sakai had purchased carpet and had it installed in the entrance of the Beverly Hills house. The witnesses said the new carpet was a small piece that closely matched the color of the surrounding carpet in the house.

Deputy Dist. Atty. Lonnie A. Felker said Sanae Sakai's quick replacement of the rug was part of the evidence that showed she knew of the killing and was aiding her son. Sanae Sakai has denied she had anything to do with her husband's killing.

MURDER CASE

Tough choices in deal for crucial testimony.

June 1, 1988

Police were able to break open the Takashi Sakai murder case because one of the men who took part in the killing made a mistake: He left a fingerprint on a parking lot ticket when he left the dead man's car at Los Angeles International Airport.

But the man who left the fingerprint, 21-year-old Greg Meier, will not face a day in jail for his role in the murder, although he admitted that he helped ambush the wealthy Japanese businessman, club him with a steel pipe and bury the body after Sakai had been stabbed to death.

Using the fingerprint as the key piece of evidence gathered in a 10-month investigation of Sakai's disappearance, authorities in February persuaded Meier to tell what happened to the missing Tarzana man and lead them to his body.

In exchange for that help and for agreeing to testify about the murder, Meier was granted immunity from prosecution. He is now expected to be the key witness in the prosecution of his best friend, Toru Sakai, 21, who is charged with murder and conspiracy in the fatal stabbing of his father.

Meier is also expected to play an important role as a witness in the prosecution of the dead man's widow, Sanae Sakai, who is charged with being an accessory to murder.

The granting of immunity to Meier points out the frustrations authorities faced in solving what they called an almost-perfect crime.

Deputy Dist. Atty. Lonnie A. Felker, who will prosecute the Sakais, is not happy that Meier will avoid prosecution but said there was little choice. Evidence gathered against Meier might not have been sufficient to convict him of participating in the murder, Felker said, but the information he provided after receiving immunity was critical in bringing charges against the man believed to be the actual killer, Toru Sakai.

"Unfortunately, we had to let someone go without

any jail time," Felker said. "There was nothing else we could do.

"It was a choice between everybody going free and seeing just one go free. We didn't want the person who actually inflicted the fatal blows to Takashi Sakai to walk away. Toru was the one we wanted."

But the prosecution of Toru Sakai will have to wait until he is found by police. His whereabouts have been unknown since he fled from the family home in Tarzana while Meier was cooperating with authorities. Meanwhile, his mother has pleaded innocent in Los Angeles Superior Court.

Takashi (Glenn) Sakai, 54, a founder of Pacific Partners, an affiliate of World Trade Bank in Beverly Hills, disappeared April 20, 1987. Police from the outset believed he was the victim of foul play. They said it was hard to believe Sakai would leave behind a successful career as an adviser to Japanese businesses seeking to invest in the United States.

Investigators soon learned that Sakai was in the midst of a divorce and that there were bitter feelings with his son and 51-year-old wife, a one-time Japanese beauty contest winner and a descendant of one of the top five families of Japan's pre-1945 nobility.

Two days after the disappearance, Sakai's Mercedes-Benz was found parked at Los Angeles International Airport. Police found no signs that he had taken a flight from the airport and only one clue to what happened to him: the fingerprint on the airport parking ticket stub that had been left in the car.

During the next several months, the investigation moved slowly. Sakai's body had not been found, and police had no match for the fingerprint.

Then, in November, the operator of a private mailbox company in Hollywood where Takashi Sakai had kept a box told Los Angeles police that a young man had come in, presented the key and requested access to it. The man left when he was turned down because he was not Sakai, but the business operator wrote down the license plate number of the car he was driving.

Detectives Jerry Le Frois and Jay Rush traced the car to Greg Meier of San Marino.

Close Friends

According to authorities, Meier and Toru Sakai were close friends who had met at San Marino High School when they played tennis together. Both were known as quiet youths who did not participate in many school activities. Tennis and a shared interest in becoming musicians made the basis of their friendship.

Beneath his senior photo in the 1983 Titanian yearbook, Toru Sakai skipped the inspirational messages most students chose and placed a bleakly pessimistic quote attributed to Mick Jagger:

"There've been good times; there've been bad times; I've had my share of hard times too, but I lost my faith in the world. . . ."

Beneath Meier's photo, the caption he chose read, "If you don't get life, life will get you."

The friendship lasted well after high school and the Sakai family's move from San Marino to Tarzana. The two briefly attended UCLA together and later worked occasionally doing renovation and maintenance work on homes that Sanae Sakai managed for Japanese investors.

After tracing the license number to Meier, investigators asked him to come to police headquarters to answer questions and be fingerprinted. Meier complied and was released. There was not enough evidence to charge him with a crime.

Print Matches

By early February, however, police had matched one of Meier's fingerprints to the print on the parking stub.

Investigators took Meier into custody on Feb. 9, this time telling him that the fingerprint and other evidence added up to probable cause to charge him, Felker said.

"We confronted him," the prosecutor recalled. "He indicated he might be able to help us."

Meier consulted an attorney and then offered to tell what happened in exchange for immunity. Felker said that with no body, no crime scene, no motive for Meier to kill Sakai and little other evidence beyond the fingerprint, authorities had no choice.

"We concurred — it was the only way to go," said Lt. Ron Lewis, who supervised the Los Angeles police investigation of the case. "I can't imagine that any law enforcement officer would be too happy about an individual being allowed to walk away, but you have to take in the total picture. Certainly it bothers me, but it was our only option."

Before granting immunity, Felker said, authorities determined through investigation and discussions with Meier and his attorney that Meier had not been the one who stabbed Takashi Sakai to death.

Official Reasoning

"We assured ourselves that he was not the actual killer, and we assured ourselves that he did not initiate the thought of the killing," Felker said. "We gave him immunity because he was not the person who inflicted the fatal injuries."

The day after immunity was granted, Meier led a team of investigators to Malibu Canyon and pointed out the spot where Takashi Sakai had been buried 10 months earlier. He also provided details of the murder that had frustrated investigators for just as long.

Those details were revealed publicly for the first time last week when Meier testified at Sanae Sakai's preliminary hearing. His audience included more than two dozen Japanese journalists, there because the standing of the Sakai family and the alleged patricide, a rarity in Japan, have drawn the interest of the Japanese community here and across the Pacific.

Speaking calmly, but often exhaling nervously into the microphone, Meier said that Toru Sakai talked on and off of wanting to kill his father for three months in early 1987. He said the talks often occurred while the two friends cruised in Toru's Porsche over the Santa Monica Mountains or dined and drank in Westwood restaurants near UCLA.

Bitter Divorce

According to Meier and authorities, Toru Sakai wanted to kill his father because his parents were embroiled in a bitter divorce and he feared that he and his mother would face financial difficulties.

"He told me, basically, that he hated his father, and he didn't know what else to do," Meier testified.

On April 20, 1987, according to Meier, Toru lured his father to a vacant home in Beverly Hills that Sanae Sakai managed for an investor. Meier said he was standing behind the front door with a steel pipe in his hand when the older Sakai walked in.

"He took a couple steps in, and I came up behind him," Meier said. "I was successful in hitting him in the neck, but he didn't go down. For some reason, I thought I would be able to knock him out — like in the movies. But it doesn't work that way."

There was a bloody struggle and Takashi Sakai was struck several more times by his son and Meier before being subdued, handcuffed and pushed down the basement stairs, prosecutors said.

"He was moaning and yelling for help at the bottom of the stairs," said Meier, who testified that Toru Sakai then asked him to kill his father.

"He went over to a bag and pulled out a big knife," Meier said. "He asked me to go down and finish him off."

Buried Body

Meier said he refused, so Toru Sakai went down and killed the elder Sakai. The two friends then wrapped the body in a rug, Meier testified, and loaded it into Toru's Porsche. They drove to Malibu Canyon, he said, and buried the body before returning to the Beverly Hills house the next day to get rid of evidence and paint over the blood-spattered walls.

Meier told investigators that when he drove the dead man's car to Los Angeles International Airport the day after the murder, he wore gloves so that there would be no fingerprints left in the car. But when he had to reach out the window to take the parking stub, he took the gloves off so that he would not look suspicious. After he got the stub, he put the gloves back on and rubbed the stub to erase any fingerprints, he said.

"But the oil from one of his fingers had already been absorbed into the paper," Felker said. "The print stayed there. It was the one thing" that connected him with Takashi Sakai's disappearance.

Several months later, when Meier confessed his role in the murder to authorities, he added one other grim detail to an already gruesome case, Felker said.

Meier told investigators that he and Toru Sakai returned to Malibu Canyon about two months after the murder and partially dug up Takashi Sakai's body. Toru Sakai used a pair of shears to cut a finger off the body so he could remove a gold ring. Then the body was reburied.

A year later, Felker said, the case has placed authorities in the uncomfortable situation of having to choose for whom justice would be served.

"Our only concern is that at the end of this thing justice is done for as many people as possible," Felker said. "On a professional level, I do not feel badly about it because I am doing what needs to be done to make sure justice is done.

"On a personal level, I feel badly that everyone that is involved cannot be prosecuted. It is a terrible thing to see some person who is involved just walk away."

Although Meier faces no criminal charges in the Sakai case, he does face his own guilt, the prosecutor noted.

"I don't really know how to judge how much he feels remorse," Felker said. "I know he feels badly about it. He has told me about it several times. The murder wasn't reality to him until it happened. He was so deeply involved then that he had to stay involved."

Meier could not be reached for comment. But during his testimony last week, he momentarily faltered while being questioned about the murder.

"This is tough," he said. "It's tough, emotionally."

SUSPECT REMAINS AT LARGE ALMOST 2 YEARS AFTER HIS FATHER'S SLAYING

Toru Sakai was held in 1987 after his father's death, but was released for lack of evidence. Now police say they have a case, but the suspect is gone.

November 6, 1989

On Dec. 3, 1987, Los Angeles police had Toru Sakai right where they wanted him: in a North Hollywood jail cell, under arrest on suspicion of his father's murder.

But the one thing they didn't have at the time was the body of his father, Takashi Sakai, a wealthy Japanese businessman who had lived in Tarzana. Without the body or any other conclusive evidence that a murder had occurred, Toru Sakai, then 21, was released uncharged after two days in jail.

The police never got another chance to arrest the diminutive former UCLA student. By the time investigators found the victim's body and the evidence they needed to charge his son with the slaying, Toru Sakai had vanished.

Today, after nearly two years of sifting through more than 500 leads and traveling as far as Washington in one direction and Tokyo in the other, investigators say they have no clue as to Toru Sakai's exact whereabouts. They say one of Los Angeles' most notable crimes in recent years remains at an unusual standstill. It has been solved, police say. But the suspect remains free.

"We are still looking for Toru, we still get clues," said Detective Jay Rush. "But he is in the wind. . . .

"It is frustrating when you know who killed someone and why, but you can't catch him. It is more frustrating than an unsolved case."

The Takashi Sakai case was unsolved for most of 1987. The 54-year-old founder of the Beverly Hills–based Pacific Partners, a subsidiary of World Trade Bank, disappeared after leaving his office April 20, 1987.

At first the case was handled as a missing person investigation, but detectives quickly suspected foul play. They regarded the sudden disappearance of Sakai, who used the name Glenn in the United States, as unusual, because he was in the middle of a major business deal. His Mercedes-Benz was found at Los Angeles International Airport, but a fingerprint found on the parking stub was not his.

Because Sakai, a former president of the Little Tokyo Chamber of Commerce, was well known and influential in international business circles, authorities theorized he might have been kidnapped. The missing person case was turned over to the Robbery-Homicide Division, which handles kidnappings.

After finding no evidence of an abduction, Detectives Rush and Jerry Le Frois turned their attention to Sakai's family. In the previous year the missing man had moved out of his family's hillside home in Tarzana and was divorcing his wife, Sanae Sakai, a descendant of Japanese nobility and former beauty pageant queen. At the time of his disappearance, he was living in the Hollywood Hills.

Investigators said the marriage was not ending amicably, and Toru Sakai had sided with his mother in a bitter dispute with his father over money. The detectives believed that dispute was the motivation behind the elder Sakai's disappearance.

"Glenn Sakai had told people that if anything ever happened to him, his wife and son would be at fault," Le Frois said.

But the investigators lacked evidence. The break in the case didn't come until November 1987, when a man with Glenn Sakai's key to a private mail deposit box in Hollywood attempted to collect mail from the box. The man was turned away because he was not Sakai, but the operator of the mail drop got the license plate number from his car.

The tag number was traced to Gregory Meier, a former classmate and tennis partner of Toru Sakai. Meier told police he had gotten the mailbox key from Toru, and that led to Toru's arrest on Dec. 3, 1987, on suspicion of murder. But with no body, no crime scene and little other evidence, no charges were filed and he was released.

However, two months later, after police had matched Meier's fingerprint to the LAX ticket stub, Meier agreed to cooperate in exchange for immunity. He said Glenn Sakai was stabbed to death by his son after being lured to an unoccupied Beverly Hills mansion, which was managed for its absentee owner by Sanae Sakai. Meier, who said he took part in the attack but did not inflict the fatal wounds, led police to the executive's grave in Malibu Canyon.

On Feb. 10, 1988, police once again went to the Sakai house to arrest Toru, but he was gone. They arrested Sanae Sakai, and she was charged as an accessory to murder after the fact. Authorities said she helped her son cover up the crime.

The charge against Sanae Sakai was dropped, and she has repeatedly denied any knowledge of the crime or of her son's whereabouts.

The only trace of Toru Sakai police believe may be credible was an anonymous call in early 1988 from a woman who knew unpublished details about the Sakai family and the case and told investigators that Toru had left the country by crossing the Canadian border to Vancouver.

But authorities say that if the suspect did leave the country, it was without his passport, which had been confiscated when he was arrested in 1987. Still, authorities believe Sakai might have been able to get to Japan from Vancouver. Clues phoned to detectives from the Japanese community in Los Angeles as recently as a month ago place the fugitive in Japan, Le Frois said. "We assume he could have gotten a passport and gotten to Japan," the detective said.

Toru Sakai was born in Japan, but he left with his family for California when he was 1 year old. Investigators said he spoke Japanese poorly and as a teen-ager had had plastic surgery to westernize his eyes — factors that might make him noticeable in Japan.

However, there has never been a confirmed sighting of Sakai in Japan or anywhere else, authorities said. The lack of viable clues to his whereabouts is unusual. Investigators say fugitives often are tracked by their mistakes; using credit cards or passports, telephone records, giving a real Social Security number or leaving fingerprints while using false names.

"Usually there is some kind of a trail," said Los Angeles County Deputy Dist. Atty. Lonnie A. Felker, who filed the murder charge against Toru Sakai. "But on this one there is no trail. Japan is a possibility. But so is Canada. He could still be here. We don't know."

Detectives went to Tokyo and provided law enforcement officials with details of the case, which was highly publicized there because of the stature of the Sakai family and rarity of patricide in Japan.

Investigators also went to Washington to take telephone calls from tipsters after details of the case, photos of Toru Sakai and mention of his love for tennis and his use of the name Chris were aired twice on the television show *America's Most Wanted*. The exposure from the program, which was also translated and televised in Japan, brought hundreds of tips. They led to at least nine different states and Japan, but none led to the real Toru Sakai.

A tip that came from Palm Springs seemed the most promising. The caller said an Asian man was living in a secluded condominium in the desert community. The man went by the name Chris, didn't seem to work and often played tennis at the complex.

"Everything fit," Le Frois said. Photos were sent to Palm Springs police, who checked out the tip. The report back was that there was a very close resemblance. It could be Toru Sakai.

Palm Springs police moved in and detained the man after pulling him out of a condominium swimming pool. In the meantime, Rush and Le Frois headed to Palm Springs with a copy of their suspect's fingerprints. They knew as soon as they got there they had the wrong man. The man pulled from the pool was too tall. Then the fingerprint check confirmed he wasn't Toru Sakai.

"It's just cold," Le Frois said of their suspect's trail.

Authorities say the search for Toru Sakai remains

active and that the detectives meet regularly with Felker, the deputy district attorney, to update the status of the case. But for the most part, they acknowledge that they are still waiting for the call that leads them to the suspected killer, or for him to make a mistake.

"He could make a mistake," Rush said. "He could get arrested for something else and a fingerprint could be taken. . . ."

"He is out there somewhere," the detective added wistfully. "And he is probably looking over his shoulder. . . . He better be looking over his shoulder for me."

NOTE: Toru Sakai has never been captured. His whereabouts remain unknown.

WIFE KILLER

DAUGHTER SAYS FATHER,
WIFE HE'S ACCUSED OF
KILLING HAD ARGUED

LOS ANGELES TIMES
January 15, 1991

Michael J. Hardy, accused of murdering his wife and burying her body in his backyard five years ago, argued with the victim for hours the day she disappeared, the defendant's daughter testified in Van Nuys Municipal Court on Monday.

Cheryl Hardy also said she saw that her stepmother, Deborah Hardy, had been temporarily knocked unconscious during the argument at the couple's Canoga Park home on Thanksgiving Day 1985.

Her testimony came during a preliminary hearing on the murder charge against Michael Hardy, 46, who has pleaded not guilty.

Hardy, now of La Jolla, was arrested Nov. 2 after Los Angeles police unearthed a body, later identified as Deborah Hardy, in the backyard of the former Hardy home in the 20600 block of Sherman Way.

Police were acting on a tip from the suspect's 25-year-old son, Robert, who told investigators that his father enlisted him to help bury his stepmother after the elder Hardy had killed her by striking her with a flashlight.

Police said the son, a California prison inmate, told them that he had been bothered by the crime for years. He does not face charges.

Michael Hardy, an unemployed actor, was described as a mob hit man in an appearance on the TV show *Geraldo* and in a 1977 profile in *New York* magazine. Los Angeles police said they have no evidence linking him to other killings.

In court Monday, Judith Samuel, executive director of the Haven Hills shelter for battered women, said that on the day before Thanksgiving 1985, Deborah Hardy came to the shelter, saying she and her daughter, Cheryl, had been beaten by her husband. Samuel said they left after being told that authorities would be contacted.

Cheryl Hardy, now of San Diego, testified that on Thanksgiving Day, she emerged from her room to find her stepmother unconscious on the floor.

Cheryl Hardy said her stepmother later regained consciousness but the next day was gone. When she asked her father what happened, "he said that she had left," Cheryl Hardy testified.

Michael Hardy, held without bail in Van Nuys Jail, has three prior felony convictions for assault with a deadly weapon, child stealing and assault on a police officer with a firearm.

According to court records, Deborah Hardy sought a restraining order in 1985 to keep her husband away from her, claiming he had broken seven of her ribs, damaged her spleen and beaten her daughter.

TRIAL ORDERED FOR MAN ACCUSED OF KILLING WIFE, BURYING HER IN YARD

January 16, 1991

A La Jolla man was ordered Tuesday to stand trial on charges he murdered his wife five years ago and buried her in the backyard of their former home in Canoga Park.

Michael J. Hardy will stand trial in the death of his wife, Deborah L. Hardy, after a Los Angeles police detective testified at a preliminary hearing in Van Nuys Municipal Court that Hardy had admitted to police that his wife suffered a fatal head injury when he pushed her during an argument.

After police unearthed her body last year behind their former Sherman Way home and arrested him, Hardy told investigators that they had been arguing on Thanksgiving Day 1985 when she grabbed a gun and fired into the floor, Detective Phil Quartararo testified.

In a tape-recorded interview, Hardy said he then pushed her and she struck her head, the detective testified.

"He said he slapped the gun away," Quartararo testified. "He said he pushed her away and she became unconscious" after hitting her head against a wall or table.

Hardy, 46, told police his wife died hours later without regaining consciousness and he asked his son, Robert, to help bury the body, the detective said.

Quartararo said that in a second interview with police, Hardy changed details of the story, saying that his wife fired the gun into the ceiling.

The Hardy family later moved from Canoga Park to La Jolla. The body was not discovered until Nov. 2, 1990, when Robert Hardy, now 25 and an inmate in a California prison, told police about the burial.

The son told investigators that his father had told him

he killed Deborah Hardy by hitting her with a flashlight, Quartararo said.

In earlier testimony, Hardy's 22-year-old daughter, Cheryl Hardy, testified that her stepmother had fired a shot into the ceiling about a week before the Thanksgiving Day argument.

Deputy Dist. Atty. Marsh M. Goldstein told Municipal Judge Robert L. Swasey that the evidence indicated Deborah Hardy did not threaten her husband with a gun at the time she was killed.

At the conclusion of testimony, Hardy's attorney, Randall Megee, failed to persuade Swasey to dismiss the murder charge or reduce it to manslaughter.

Hardy is an unemployed actor who was described as a mob hit man during an appearance last year on the television show *Geraldo* and in a 1977 profile in *New York* magazine. Los Angeles police said they have found no evidence linking him to other killings.

SELF-PROMOTING 'CONTRACT KILLER' ENTERS PLEA TO KILLING WIFE IN '85

August 17, 1991

A La Jolla man who fostered what police called an unfounded media reputation as a mob "hit man" pleaded no contest Friday to a charge that he killed his wife six years ago during a Thanksgiving Day argument and buried her in the backyard of their former Canoga Park home.

Michael J. Hardy, 46, entered the plea — equivalent to a guilty plea under California criminal law — in Van Nuys Superior Court to a charge of voluntary manslaughter in the 1985 death of his wife, Deborah L. Hardy, 31.

The victim's remains were uncovered behind a house on Sherman Way last year when Michael Hardy's 25-year-old son, Robert, who is serving a prison term for burglary, told police about the killing and provided a map detailing where he had helped his father bury the body.

Hardy was characterized in a 1977 *New York* magazine article and more recently on the *Geraldo* television show as an organized-crime hit man who had killed 14 people. Police have said, however, that although Hardy has a lengthy criminal record, they don't believe he was ever a mob hit man.

Hardy faces up to 11 years in prison when sentenced next month by Judge Judith M. Ashmann. Hardy, who had been charged with murder, could have been sentenced to 42 years if his case went to trial and he was convicted, so he decided to plead no contest to the lesser charge, said his attorney, James E. Blatt.

"He didn't want to take the chance of going to prison for the rest of his life," Blatt said.

Exactly how Deborah Hardy was killed on Thanksgiving Day 1985 may never be known because autopsy results were inconclusive and Hardy himself is the only witness to the death, said Deputy Dist. Atty. Marsh Goldstein, who handled the case.

Robert Hardy, who said he helped bury the body but did not see the slaying, told police that his father admitted to him that he killed his wife with a blow from a flashlight.

But after his arrest, the elder Hardy claimed in statements to police that his wife was fatally injured when he pushed her as she threatened him with a gun.

Because of those inconsistencies and the couple's record of violent fights resulting in police reports, the prosecution agreed to a manslaughter plea, Goldstein said.

"While there are overtones of murder, the essence of this case is that they had a long history of problems and he hit her too hard, and that is manslaughter," Goldstein said.

Blatt said that even if Hardy receives the maximum 11-year sentence, he could be released from prison in five years with time off for good conduct and the year he has already been in jail.

Hardy had three prior felony convictions for assault with a deadly weapon, child stealing and assault on a police officer with a firearm.

In a 1977 profile in *New York* magazine, Hardy boasted of having committed 800 car thefts and 250 robberies and having connections to organized crime. The article also indicated that he was involved in 14 contract slayings. Last year, Hardy appeared in disguise on Geraldo Rivera's syndicated television show during a segment on purported hit men. He declined to confirm or deny his involvement in the slayings when Rivera questioned him.

"I'm not going to sit here on national TV and confess to murders because, you know, you really aren't paying me enough for that," said Hardy, who used the name Michael Hardin on the program.

Authorities said they found no indications that Hardy was actually a contract killer.

"I think he's a blowhard," Goldstein said. "He has lived a long and violent life, but no hit man worth his salt goes around talking about it."

THE GANG THAT COULDN'T SHOOT STRAIGHT

THE MAIL-ORDER MURDERS

SOUTH FLORIDA SUN-SENTINEL
October 4, 1987

IT WOULD HAVE BEEN comical if it hadn't been so deadly, if lives hadn't been mercilessly ended or, at the very least, haunted by terror. They were called the gang that couldn't shoot straight, yet they were a gang that had so many shots, they were bound to hit their targets sometimes, and people were bound to die.

For months they tried to kill Doug Norwood, but

whether they came at him with machine guns or bombs or stun guns, they always managed to screw up. The same thing with Dana Free. Three times they missed. And when it came time to kill Victoria Barshear, well, the gang just decided she was too pretty to die.

Those were some of the gaffes that made them laughable. But there was nothing laughable about what happened to Richard Braun and Anita Spearman. They killed Braun, though it took two tries, in the front yard of his home. It took only one visit from the gang and Anita Spearman was left dead in her bed.

They were want-ad killers, a gang of losers, social outcasts and law enforcement washouts headed by a man with the seemingly appropriate name of Richard Savage. They picked their targets from West Palm Beach to St. Paul, their clients from the Atlantic to the Rockies.

It was nothing personal. In a sleazy Tennessee bar where strippers danced, the gang plotted the deaths of people they had never even seen: Anita Spearman, the well-known and well-liked assistant city manager in West Palm Beach; Doug Norwood, a law student in Arkansas; Dana Free, a contractor in Georgia. And others, many others.

THEY PICTURED THEMSELVES as guns for hire. One day barroom bouncers, the next day cross-country contract killers. No job too big or too small. One member helped a man put a bomb on a plane loaded with 154 people. One shot down a man in his driveway while his son watched in horror. Another threw grenades into a home where a 14-year-old and his mother were sleeping.

Their crimes were spread across the country, to avoid a pattern of terror that might aid the police in their investigations. What did the bombing of a businessman's van in Atlanta have to do with a suitcase explosion in the cargo hold of a jet in Dallas? What could the arson of a poultry plant in Iowa have in common with the murder of a city official in Palm Beach County?

Seemingly, the answer would be nothing, the questions not even considered. Even so, in less than a year, a far-flung network of investigative agencies working on the many separate cases found the common denominator in the back pages of a magazine published for gun and battle buffs. From there the investigators picked up the pieces of the puzzle and put it together. Even today, they feel lucky about it.

"This is a case of truth being stranger than fiction — it's mind-boggling," says Tom Stokes, special agent in charge of the Atlanta office of the federal Bureau of Alcohol, Tobacco and Firearms (ATF). "At times you needed a flow chart to keep it straight. These guys were bouncing all over the country doing these jobs. Thank goodness, we got coordinated on it."

In the end, two people were dead, several others were injured, and many were scared for their lives. Doug

Norwood, who escaped death three times after being shot and bombed, still carries a gun. Who can blame him? Across the country Savage's gang had left a trail of terror and deadly ineptitude.

THE TRAIL STARTED in spring 1985 in Knoxville, Tenn. Richard Savage was into his fourth business venture in almost as many years and there was no telling whether his Continental Club was going to do any better than the restaurant or the motel or the nursing home that had failed before it.

Savage's new profession — operator of a rundown strip bar — was his strangest yet. It seemed so far from the way he had started out. Born in Knoxville 37 years before, he had joined the Army out of high school, serving for six years, including a tour in Vietnam as a courier. When he left the military he decided to put on a new uniform, that of a cop.

However, Savage found no lasting promise in the new uniform. After earning a criminal justice degree in Kentucky, he worked only briefly as a cop in Oklahoma, then as a federal prison guard in Lexington, Ky. He bounced around the Midwest and by 1980 had drifted into his series of failed business ventures.

By 1985, Savage was determined to put the skills he had learned in his previous careers to good use. He decided to put himself out for hire.

The back pages of *Soldier of Fortune* magazine are devoted to classified ads offering a whole raft of goods and services to what the magazine calls the "professional adventurer." On any given month this marketplace might offer anything from countersurveillance information to mercenary manuals to handbooks on revenge.

But in the early 1980s, the *Soldier of Fortune* classified ads offered more sinister services. Investigators have said it was through ads placed here that a variety of hired killers advertised their lethal skills. And it was into this market that Richard Savage placed his own skills the summer of 1985:

Gun For Hire: 37-year-old professional mercenary desires jobs. Vietnam Veteran. Discrete [sic] *and very private. Body Guard, Courier and other Skills. All jobs considered.*

Sylvester Stallone, portraying Rambo, was on the cover of the magazine's June issue in which Savage's "Gun For Hire" ad promised that all jobs would be considered. The ad carried the telephone number of the Continental Club, and within days the phone was ringing with inquiries.

The calls were from people both looking to hire and looking for work. By midsummer Savage had surrounded himself with a cadre of men seeking dial-a-gun work. There was 21-year-old Sean Doutre, a knockabout who signed on as a bouncer at the Continental Club.

There was Michael Wayne Jackson, 42, the one-time police chief of a tiny Texas town but now a maintenance man. There was William Buckley, 35, a local security guard. And there were others — all men who apparently found the macho image of themselves reflected in the action stories and ads of *Soldier of Fortune*.

Other callers were clients looking for a variety of questionable jobs done. Savage was asked to guard gold in Alaska, to find men still missing in Vietnam. But for the most part, people called because they wanted someone killed.

"I couldn't believe it," Savage would tell a *News/Sun-Sentinel* reporter a year after his ad ran. "Nearly everybody wanted someone killed. They wanted me to kill their wives, mothers, fathers and girlfriends."

According to investigators, indictments and court records, Savage and his gang entered into deadly agreements with a number of the callers. The going rate was $20,000 a kill.

Investigators believe that within a few weeks of his ad in *Soldier of Fortune,* Savage had accepted the first assignment and dispatched a crew of hit men to suburban Atlanta to kill a 43-year-old businessman named Richard Braun. On June 9, an explosive device was placed in Braun's van, but it exploded before Braun got in the vehicle. The bombers would make up for missing him two months later.

The second job was in Fertile, Iowa. A St. Paul,

Minn., bar owner named Richard Lee Foster had called Savage, claiming that the Keough Poultry Company in Fertile had ripped him off. Savage assigned Michael Wayne Jackson and William Buckley to the Foster case, and on the night of June 23 an explosion ripped through the Keough plant. No one was hurt, but Foster got his revenge — for the time being.

By EARLY AUGUST, the dial-a-hit-man crew was back in Georgia, this time in Marietta to kill a building contractor named Dana Free. Savage had been paid $20,000 by a Denver woman angry at Free over a failed business investment. But killing Free wasn't easy.

On Aug. 1, Buckley and Jackson planted two grenades under Free's car. Free drove around with the devices under his car for a day but nothing happened, partly because the pin on one of the grenades had not been removed. So the next night, Buckley slid under the car and reattached the grenades with their pins tied to the drive shaft. If the car moved, the pins would be yanked out and . . . kaboom!

In the morning, Free got in and as he started to pull out of his driveway, he saw a grenade, pin still attached, roll out from under the car. He managed to jump from the vehicle before the other grenade blew up. He was uninjured — and lucky. He went into hiding.

Next, it was back to the Midwest. Bar owner Richard

Lee Foster had been impressed enough with Savage's handling of his complaint with the Keough company to sign on for another job. But this time the results weren't as good. Over three nights beginning Aug. 10, members of the gang planted an assortment of bombs in Harry's 63 Club, a St. Paul bar competing with Foster's. None of the devices functioned properly, and for the first two nights the bombers crept back into the bar to remove them. On the third night, with the bomb smoking and setting off alarms, the police bomb squad beat them to it.

"They just couldn't get it right," says ATF special agent Tom Stokes. "They were like the gang that couldn't shoot straight or think straight. Sometimes you had to wonder if this whole thing wasn't a comedy of errors."

ON AUG. 26, the comical bumbling ended. On that day, according to investigators, Savage sent Doutre back to Georgia and, for the first time, the gang struck with deadly accuracy. Richard Braun, who had escaped death once before, was machine-gunned as he drove his Mercedes-Benz out of his driveway. Braun's 16-year-old son, who was also in the car, was slightly wounded and watched his father bleed to death.

The want-ad killers next took an assignment from an Arkansas man named Larry Gray, who wanted his ex-wife's boyfriend, a Fayetteville law student named Doug Norwood, eliminated.

Four days after the Braun killing, Norwood answered the door of his apartment and two men came at him with an electric-charged stun gun. Norwood escaped after punching one and throwing the other through a glass door, but was wounded by gunfire as he fled from his apartment. He ran to a car parked nearby and asked a man standing next to it for help.

"He just looked at me, slowly got into the car and drove away," Norwood recalls.

That was because Norwood had stumbled up to his assailants' getaway driver, a man he would later come to know as Richard Savage. Norwood then ran into a nearby Laundromat and called the police. His attackers, later identified as William Buckley and another Savage associate named Dean DeLuca, managed to escape.

Norwood had no idea why he was being attacked or who was after him. He bought a .357 Magnum and started carrying it wherever he went. However, the weapon didn't help him much on Oct. 1. That afternoon, when he turned the ignition key in his car in a University of Arkansas parking lot, a bomb beneath his car partially exploded. The car was destroyed but Norwood escaped without injury.

While some members of the gang waited for another chance to get Norwood, others were working on new assignments.

In Lexington, Ky., investigators say a woman named Mary Alice Wolf hired Savage to kill her ex-husband's new wife, Victoria Barshear. Savage sent Doutre, Buckley and DeLuca to do the job but it never got done. After seeing Barshear, the hired killers decided she was too pretty to kill and left town.

But Dana Free was still unfinished business. And at 3 a.m. on Oct. 12, William Buckley, the man who had already messed up earlier chances at Free, as well as Norwood and Barshear, threw two grenades into a house in Pasadena, Tex. No one was hurt in the explosion, and Free wasn't even there. The home belonged to his ex-wife and 14-year-old son, who were inside asleep when the grenades came crashing through the living room window.

The gang's next assignment was potentially the most lethal they ever attempted. On Oct. 30, at Dallas/Fort Worth International Airport, an American Airlines flight from Austin, with 154 people on board, was taxiing toward the terminal when a small bomb exploded in the luggage hold. Passengers were rushed off the plane, scared but unhurt.

Investigators found the remains of a time bomb in luggage belonging to passenger Mary Theilman. She had been meant to die, presumably along with the rest of the passengers. A month later, authorities charged Theilman's husband, Albert, with the crime. It would be a year before they would charge William Buckley with selling him the bomb.

• • •

IN OCTOBER, Richard Savage began receiving calls from a man in Palm Beach County, Florida. The man, Robert Spearman, said that he had this problem. He was married and didn't want to be. But he didn't want a divorce.

On Oct. 16, Savage flew to Palm Beach to meet Spearman and take a $2,000 down payment on a $20,000 contract to kill Spearman's 48-year-old wife, Anita. Five days later, Savage sent Sean Doutre and Ronald Emert, another associate from the Continental Club, to West Palm Beach to collect the balance.

In the weeks after Doutre and Emert left with the money, Robert Spearman placed several more calls to the Continental Club. Authorities would later charge that these were calls to find out what was happening on the deal and to demand quick service from Savage.

Whatever they were for, Spearman no longer needed to call after the early hours of Nov. 16. On that morning, after Spearman had exited his Palm Beach Gardens home to drop by his marine contracting company's office, Sean Doutre entered the house through an unlocked door and found Anita Spearman, who was recovering from a mastectomy, asleep. Doutre beat her to death as she lay on her bed.

A short time later, Robert Spearman came home to find his wife dead and the house ransacked. He quickly called the sheriff's department, portraying himself as a grieving husband. It was an act authorities would not take long to see through.

THERE WERE ALL these victims, all these bizarre crimes, but seemingly nothing that linked them. This widespread dispersal of investigative effort should have insured the gang's getaway. But it wasn't to be. For in addition to having bungled many of their murder attempts, the hit men had operated in a way that belied the very promises of their classified ad.

The ad stated they would be discreet and very private. But they had rented cars, kept receipts, made long-distance phone calls, made themselves memorable to witnesses. They ran out on bills, kept stolen weapons and carried large quantities of cash. They left high-powered weapons displayed on the seats of their cars. And most of all, they talked too much.

This is how discreet and private Sean Doutre was: The day after he killed Anita Spearman, he was stopped by police in Maryville, Tenn., for a traffic violation. On the backseat of his car was a 12-gauge shotgun stolen from Spearman's house the morning of the murder.

The case of the want-ad killers probably could have been broken with Doutre's arrest. But when officers checked the serial number of the shotgun against a national computer index of stolen property, they drew a blank. In Palm Beach County, the murder was only a day old and the serial number of the stolen shotgun had not yet been entered in the computer's data bank.

But Doutre did at least put investigators hard on the trail of Richard Savage. Along with the shotgun, Maryville police had found a submachine gun in Doutre's car. The weapon automatically meant that the nearest AFT office would be called to see if anybody wanted to question Doutre.

Grant McGarrity, a Knoxville agent, visited Doutre in jail that afternoon. Doutre was talkative, volunteering that he worked for a man named Savage who was in the business of sending people out on contract murders. Of course, Doutre denied that he had committed a crime himself.

It was interesting information. McGarrity had heard of Richard Savage and was already gathering information about weapons being mailed to and from the Continental Club.

Because Doutre said nothing that incriminated himself, he was able to post bond on the weapons charge and leave Maryville. However, the stolen shotgun remained behind in the police department's evidence lockup.

WHILE ALL THIS was happening, Doug Norwood, the Arkansas law student, was still scared and looking over his shoulder. Police were making little headway in their investigations of the shooting and bombing that had nearly killed him. Nor were they listening to his theory that his girlfriend's ex-husband had put hit men on his trail.

Nevertheless, Norwood's wariness eventually helped save him a third time, and helped break open the case. On Jan. 20, 1986, Norwood grew suspicious of a car that followed him to the university, and called the two campus detectives who were investigating the bombing.

The police stopped the car and began talking to its driver, Michael Wayne Jackson. One officer spotted the barrel of a gun protruding from beneath a sweater on the front seat. Jackson was arrested and police confiscated several guns, including a semiautomatic rifle.

"There is no doubt in my mind," says Norwood, "that Jackson was going to spray me with that machine gun."

Jackson proved to be as talkative as Sean Doutre. He told police that he and Savage had been hired by Larry Gray, the ex-husband of Norwood's girlfriend, to kill Norwood. And he added that Gray had contacted them through a classified ad in *Soldier of Fortune* magazine.

THE NEXT BREAK came on Feb. 5, when Sean Doutre was arrested again near Athens, Ga., simply because he had left a nearby motel without paying his long-distance phone bill. Once again, law officers listened raptly as Doutre gave details about Savage and the murder-for-hire business.

Shortly afterward, ATF agent McGarrity decided to visit a former Savage associate named Ronald Emert, who had been jailed in Knoxville on drug charges. Emert turned out to be one more key to the puzzle. In exchange for not being charged in any murder-for-hire plot, he told McGarrity about the trip he had made to Florida with Doutre to collect money from a man named Spearman. He also told McGarrity to check with the Maryville police about a shotgun that was gathering dust in their evidence closet.

Until that point, progress had been slow in Palm Beach County on the Spearman case. Robert Spearman had stopped cooperating with the sheriff's department, and detectives were mostly waiting for a lucky break. It came after Emert's conversation with McGarrity, who retrieved the shotgun from Maryville.

Palm Beach detectives flew to Knoxville, and Emert picked Robert Spearman's face out of a lineup of photographs. Investigators then began to check records of long-distance phone calls, hotels, car rentals and other business receipts gathered from Doutre and others in the Savage gang.

Finally, the net was beginning to close. Law officers from West Palm Beach north to Minneapolis and west to Dallas gathered in Atlanta for a conference on the Savage gang. ATF designated it a national investigation.

"It all sounded so wild and far-fetched — but it was all coming back as true," recalls the ATF's Tom Stokes.

Law enforcement agencies began filing charges in the various conspiracies. Savage, Doutre, Jackson, Buckley and the others were jailed. So were many of the people who had hired them.

Among them was Robert Spearman, who walked out of a store on North Lake Boulevard in West Palm Beach on April 4 to find Palm Beach County Sheriff Richard Wille waiting with a warrant charging him with his wife's murder.

THE WANT-AD killers face a litany of murder, conspiracy and weapons charges in Florida, Georgia, Tennessee, Kentucky, Texas, Minnesota and Iowa.

Last month, the chapter involving Anita Spearman ended with Richard Savage's second-degree murder conviction in a West Palm Beach courtroom. He was sentenced to 40 years in prison. Earlier, Sean Doutre and Robert Spearman had been found guilty of first-degree murder.

In the Doug Norwood attacks, Savage, Larry Gray, William Buckley and Dean DeLuca all pleaded guilty. Savage and Doutre have been charged in the Braun killing. The grenade attacks on Dana Free resulted in charges against Savage, Michael Wayne Jackson and Buckley. Buckley has also been charged in connection with the plane bomb in Dallas. Richard Lee Foster and

Mary Alice Wolf have been convicted of conspiracies to hire the Savage gang.

Charges in other cases are still pending. So far, the guns for hire are serving prison terms ranging from five years to life.

MEANWHILE, the victims who escaped the gang's deadly ineptitude are trying to return to normalcy — if that is possible.

Doug Norwood says it isn't.

He completed law school this year and is now a prosecutor for Benton County in Arkansas. He sued *Soldier of Fortune,* claiming negligence on the magazine's part in publishing the ad that led to attacks on him. He sought $4 million in damages but says he settled last month for an undisclosed amount of money. He still carries the .357 Magnum.

"I take elaborate security measures," he says. "I live in a Fort Knox. I just don't allow strangers in to talk to me and I always answer the door with my gun. I'll probably carry it until the day I die."

EVIL UNTIL HE DIES

PORTRAIT OF A
MURDER SUSPECT

Trail to Chatsworth Street is traced through the
Criminal Justice System.

LOS ANGELES TIMES
October 18, 1987

Roland Comtois knew the routine well.

Arrested by Los Angeles police on suspicion of
burglary, he hooked his glasses in the open neck of his
shirt and stared coldly at the camera. The hard set of his

eyes betrayed nothing. No fear. No concern. The camera clicked, and the mug shot was taken.

For Comtois, it was simply part of life.

Today, that June 1 mug shot is part of a history that tells much about the criminal justice system and the man accused in the abduction and shooting of two Chatsworth teen-agers last month.

Wendy Masuhara, 14, was kidnapped Sept. 19, shot in the head and killed. Her body was left in an abandoned car in a canyon six miles from the presumably safe neighborhood from which she and a 13-year-old friend had been taken.

Her friend was drugged, sexually assaulted, shot and also left for dead. But she survived and provided police with the information that identified Comtois, 58, and 33-year-old Marsha Lynn Erickson, accused of being his accomplice, as suspects. Both were familiar to police and the courts.

Comtois had woven a 46-year path through police stations, courtrooms and prisons. He was a man the criminal justice system could not handle, a man it could neither rehabilitate nor protect society from.

'Lashing Back'

"Ever since early incorrigibility," a probation officer wrote in 1962, "he has lashed back at society with a vengeance, reaching out for what he wants with a total disregard of the rights of others. . . . His personality affect is of a man who is very matter-of-fact, cold, hostile, cynical and daring."

Twenty-five years later, police describe Comtois as someone who beat the system — not because he has gotten away with crime, but because he has never gotten away *from* it. All told, records show Comtois has spent at least four stints in prison on convictions including attempted rape, robbery and heroin dealing.

And, after each sentence was served, he apparently returned to society only to lapse back into crime.

"It is not surprising that he was able to do this," Leroy Orozco, a homicide detective working full-time on Comtois' background, said last week. "His whole life has been criminal. With our justice system, people can continue to commit crimes and beat the system by continuing to get their freedom. There are people out there with worse records than he has."

Roland Norman Comtois was born in Massachusetts, the sixth of seven children of a French Canadian couple. According to court records, Comtois' mother died when he was 3, and he was placed in a succession of orphanages, foster homes and reform schools. As an adult, he would claim he was abused during this period, telling probation officers that he was punished for bed-wetting by being handcuffed and placed in cold showers. He would show scars on his wrists, claiming they were from being handcuffed as a child. Of one orphanage, he would say, "If I should ever run across the old guy who ran that place, I would blow his top off."

Comtois' education ended in the sixth grade and was followed by a Massachusetts record of juvenile delinquency that reached back as far as age 11. As a 17-year-old in 1947, he was convicted of breaking into a West Concord, Mass., lumber company office and received a two-year indeterminate sentence. How much time he served is unclear.

When Comtois was 23, a conviction for assault with intent to commit rape in New Bedford put him in a Massachusetts state prison for two years. A year after his release, he was arrested on a Peeping Tom charge, and his parole was revoked, records show.

In 1956, Comtois left a broken marriage and a daughter to move across the country. He subsequently got a divorce. In the next few years in Los Angeles, he remarried, fathered a son, worked as a truck driver and made enough money to buy a truck and begin a transport business.

But, by 1960, the business was failing, and he returned to crime. According to records, when he needed $3,200 to make repairs on the truck, he planned to rob a bank in Bell. The plan failed and he was convicted of attempted bank robbery.

When freed on bail awaiting sentencing, Comtois returned to his Los Angeles home to find his wife living on county assistance funds. Unable to find work while awaiting prison, he broke into an Alhambra home on an April morning in 1960, but was chased out of the house and slightly injured by a homeowner's bullet. Comtois was charged with burglary and pleaded guilty. "I was desperate for money . . . ," he wrote to a probation officer. "I took this spontaneous action without rational thinking."

Criminal Impulses

The probation officer's August 1960 evaluation of Comtois concluded, "He appears to have no control over his impulses when things don't go his way, and consequently he resorts to criminal behavior."

On the day his wife gave birth to a daughter, Comtois was sentenced to a year in a federal prison in California on the attempted bank robbery and burglary convictions.

Within three months of being released from prison, Comtois was jailed again, this time for the July 1961 armed robbery of a market in La Mirada. "I don't blame somebody else for what I did," he told a probation officer. "I was clear of mind." Once again he pleaded guilty to the charge. It was his fifth conviction, and he was returned to prison for his longest stay, until March 11, 1969.

Two months after his release, Comtois — half his life now spent in prisons, reform schools and orphanages — was arrested on suspicion of narcotics possession. By 1971, his wife was seeking to end their marriage. The couple separated, according to divorce documents, after Comtois flew into a Thanksgiving Day rage, punched his fist through a door in the couple's home near Long Beach and destroyed the china set on the table for the holiday meal.

The divorce records contain allegations that Comtois had often beaten his wife and had a violent temper that sent him into uncontrollable rages.

Another Failed Marriage

Two years later, Comtois would tell a judge that the end of his marriage and failures in attempts to earn a legitimate living had led him into another cycle of crime and a deep involvement with drugs. He was convicted of possession of heroin with intent to sell and of being a convicted felon in possession of a firearm. He admitted he was addicted to the drug as well.

"I started selling my jewelry and other items I owned and refused to believe I was addicted," he wrote to the judge who would sentence him. "I didn't know which way to turn. With the loss of everything, I started borrowing from business associates and friends until I had neither left.

"When I finally accepted the fact I was addicted, I started selling drugs to satisfy my addiction."

Comtois pleaded to be placed in a drug rehabilitation

program instead of prison, but the judge sent him to prison for three more years.

Comtois was released from prison in 1977 and completed parole a year later. His activities between then and last month's abduction in Chatsworth are now being documented by homicide detectives. "So far, I can't find anything legitimate about him," Detective Orozco said.

What is known is that he moved to the San Fernando Valley, possibly to be closer to his two children who lived with his ex-wife in Van Nuys.

Police said Comtois was a transient, living at an ever-changing string of addresses. He may have worked at times as a laborer, and he received a monthly disability payment for reasons unclear to police, but detectives believe he largely supported himself as a burglar and scam artist.

Some of Comtois' activities are already on record. Deputy Dist. Atty. Bradford Stone said Comtois walked into a bank in the Valley on Nov. 5, 1983, and attempted to cash a forged check for $75,000. When the teller attempted to verify the check, Comtois grabbed it back and left.

Forgery Charge

Three years later on Nov. 7, 1986, Comtois changed the date and took the same check into a bank in North

Hollywood and deposited it in his account, Stone said. During the next week he went to other banks in Los Angeles and cashed $75,000 in checks against the account. When police finally sorted it all out, he was charged March 18 of this year with grand theft and forgery.

Police say Comtois used the check scam money to buy $30,000 in gold and a new car. In January he also bought a small motor home, possibly with the same money.

Released after posting $1,500 bail, Comtois was arrested at least two more times — in June on suspicion of burglary and in July on suspicion of driving a stolen car — before the abduction. Both times he was released on bail.

By summer, Comtois was living in the brown-striped Roadstar motor home and moving freely about the Valley. Police said he was traveling with a companion, Marsha Lynn Erickson, though investigators have not discovered how or where they met.

Erickson, police say, was a Los Angeles–born transient with a record of 12 arrests in the last decade on charges including prostitution, burglary and drug possession. None of the arrests led to prison sentences. Police and court records show that she was placed on probation for at least one conviction and into drug-treatment programs after another arrest.

Erickson's father described her as a long-term heroin addict whose need for the drug overcame any attempts to help her. He spoke on the condition that he not be identified.

Companion Used Drugs

"Drugs controlled her. Drugs destroyed her," he said. "All of her problems stemmed from drugs. It was because of the heroin that she got involved in burglary and everything else. We took her to every program you could think of, but she always went back to it."

Erickson, who has had six children who were all put up for adoption, lived with her mother and father in their Chatsworth home in 1984 and 1985 while she took part in a drug-treatment program, her father said.

But, about two years ago, she left the home, about a mile from the Lurline Avenue spot where Wendy Masuhara and her friend would be kidnapped, unable to shake her dependency, her father said. Her parents have had no contact with her since, but now live with the growing nightmare that their daughter is suspected of involvement in murder.

"I can't defend her because I really don't know her anymore," her father said. "But I do find it hard to believe she could have done anything this drastic. She was always a good kid before the drugs got her."

Erickson should have been in jail the night the two girls were abducted, authorities said. Last March 16, her probation for a 1983 conviction involving $3,200 in forged checks was revoked after probation officers learned that she had been arrested twice for thefts in 1986.

A warrant for Erickson's arrest was issued, but she was never picked up by police. Chet Baker, a supervisor in the county probation department's Van Nuys office, said so many probation violation warrants are issued each year the police cannot handle them as priorities.

"The warrant goes on the computer, but other than that the police can't spend a lot of time on it," Baker said. "There are thousands of these warrants out at any one time in L.A. Plus, Erickson was a transient. Where were the police going to go to pick her up?"

Even after Erickson was arrested Aug. 19, she remained free, police said. When Northeast Division police arrested her on burglary charges, she gave a false name while being booked into jail. That allowed her to post bail before a fingerprint check identified her as Erickson and alerted police that she was wanted on the probation revocation warrant.

Month from Slaying

In less than a month, Wendy would be slain.

"If things had worked right," Baker said, "Erickson would have been sitting in jail when that took place."

Police explain the September abduction and murder as a crime of opportunity, an act of violent impulse. So far, police say, it appears that Comtois' motor home was parked that night on Lurline Avenue near Devonshire Street by coincidence. It might have simply been the spot where Comtois stopped to fix a mechanical problem in the motor home.

"Your guess is as good as mine as to why they did it," said Harold Lynn, the deputy district attorney who will prosecute Comtois and Erickson. "We don't believe they marked these particular victims for this. They just happened to be the ones that were there."

Wendy and her friend had just finished an evening of watching television at her family's home on Lurline when Wendy decided to walk her friend to her home about a block away. But, parked in their path, police said, they found Roland Comtois' motor home. Police said the girls were lured inside it when Erickson asked them for help.

Comtois, who police say shot the girls, was shot by officers and captured four days after the abduction. He is recovering but was arraigned last week on several charges in connection with the Chatsworth abduction and slaying, including murder, attempted murder, kidnapping, forcing sex acts on the surviving girl and injecting her with cocaine. He pleaded not guilty. Erickson is still at large.

The suspects could receive life imprisonment or the death penalty if convicted. But, prosecutors say, the fact that Comtois was even in a position to block the path of Wendy and her friend raised questions that some in the criminal justice system find disturbing.

Lynn, the prosecutor, said the reality of the criminal justice system is that it is not rehabilitative.

'Evil Until He Dies'

"The theory of rehabilitation is a pie-in-the-sky dream," he said. "You take a guy like Comtois, and he is evil from day one, and he is going to be evil until he dies. His record speaks for itself."

Prof. Ernest Kamm, chairman of the Department of Criminal Justice at California State University, Los Angeles, said a flaw in the way society tries to deal with someone like Comtois is in the presumption "that at one time the person was habilitated."

In fact, he said, "we find a great number of people have never adopted the mores of society in the first place. And they can't or don't want to once they return from prison."

Kamm said that, although the answer to that might be the warehousing of career criminals to keep them from society, California laws aimed at enhancing sentences for repeat offenders and putting habitual criminals permanently in prison are often circumvented.

"The reality is that there are too many holes in those laws," he said. "People can get through them."

Lynn said Comtois had to commit an aggravated crime such as he is now accused of before he could be considered under the habitual crime law. He said Comtois' previous convictions for robbery, burglary and drugs would not have applied.

Coming and Going

"Under our system, you don't do life until you do something it considers serious," Lynn said. "As long as he stayed below that line, he was one of the guys who kept coming in and going out."

Although guidelines allow longer sentences for criminals with previous convictions, it appears Comtois reduced his time in prison by pleading guilty in almost all of his convictions. When he faced the drug and weapon charges in 1974, records show that, in exchange for his guilty plea, his previous convictions were not considered at sentencing.

Finally, authorities suggest, the system is too crowded and has too few resources to give individuals the attention required for true rehabilitation or for the protection of society.

"The system cannot accommodate the intense flow of individuals," Kamm said. "Too frequently, individuals never get out of the cycle. They may wind up doing intense damage to somebody."

Roland Comtois' Criminal Record

April 1941: At age 11, he is charged with petty theft and diagnosed as an incorrigible delinquent. He is committed to reform school in Attleboro, Mass.

March 1947: Charged with breaking and entering in West Concord, Mass. He is given an indeterminate sentence limited to two years.

May 1952: Charged with assault with intent to commit rape in New Bedford, Mass. He is sentenced to three to five years in prison.

August 1955: Charged in Massachusetts in Peeping Tom incident. His parole is revoked.

February 1960: Charged with attempted bank robbery in Los Angeles. He is sentenced to one year in federal prison.

May 1960: Charged with burglary in La Mirada. His sentence is set to run concurrently with federal imprisonment.

July 1961: Charged with robbery in Los Angeles. He is sentenced to five years to life in state prison.

July 1974: Charged with possession of heroin with intent to sell and possession of a firearm by a convicted felon. He is sentenced to five years in state prison.

March 18, 1987: Charged with grand theft and forgery in Los Angeles. The case is pending.

June 1, 1987: Charged with burglary in Los Angeles. The case is pending.

July 27, 1987: Charged with car theft in Los Angeles. Case dismissed.

Sept. 24, 1987: Charged with murder, attempted murder, kidnapping and several other felonies in Los Angeles. Case is pending.

Source: Court records and probation reports

NOTE: Roland Comtois was convicted of murder and sentenced to death. In poor health because of drug abuse as well as being shot during his capture, he died in prison in 1994 while awaiting the carrying out of the sentence. Marsha Lynn Erickson was convicted of being his accomplice in the murder and was sentenced to life in prison.

PART THREE

THE CASES

NAMELESS GRAVE

IDENTITY OF MURDER VICTIM
STILL SHROUDED IN MYSTERY

SOUTH FLORIDA SUN-SENTINEL
April 14, 1986

THE GRAVE AT Hollywood Memorial Gardens has no name on it. There simply isn't one to put there. The identity of the man who is buried there is a mystery.

He was murdered March 11, 1985, in a Fort Lauderdale motel room. He was strangled. Authorities have since solved the mystery of who killed him; one man was convicted and sentenced to life in prison last week, and another suspect is being sought.

What remains to be learned is the identity of the victim.

"We don't have anything, not a clue to who he was," said Edwina Johnson, an investigator for the Broward County Medical Examiner's Office. "We have gone to great lengths to find out. We've done everything we could think of and gotten no luck whatsoever. It would seem that somebody has to know who he was."

Fort Lauderdale Police Detective Phil Mundy said that in his 10 years in the homicide bureau there have been unidentified murder victims before, but not a case where a killer is caught and convicted while the name of the victim remains unknown.

"It's unusual," he said. "In a whodunit type of murder, you first try to identify the dead man and go from there. But we never got anywhere with the identification. All we have is a dead man who has nothing extraordinary about his appearance. He could fit the description of thousands of men."

On police and medical examiner's records, the murder victim is simply known as "unidentified white male, case no. 85-43959." On court documents, photographs of the man slumped in the motel room and laid out on a medical examiner's table are attached to that identification.

The man is described as having been 5-foot-8, weighing 180 pounds, with brown hair, eyes and mustache. He was approximately 35 years old.

He was found sprawled on the floor of a room at the Interlude Motel, 1215 S. Federal Highway. Police think he accompanied two male prostitutes to the room and then was robbed and killed. His body was nude. There were no clothes or other belongings in the room. No wallet. No I.D. Just the signs of a struggle and a bloody handprint on the wall — a print that would later lead to the identification of one of his killers.

"There was nothing left in that room that could help us identify the victim," said Mundy. "The killers took it with them."

So the detective started with the dead man's fingerprints. They were sent to state and national agencies, to Canadian authorities and to Interpol for comparison. They got no matches.

Missing persons bulletins were sent out across the country with an artist's drawing of the victim attached. A few leads came back, but they were dead ends.

"Nothing panned out. They weren't our guy," said Mundy. "Usually the description wouldn't match. We ran down a few of the names we got and found each guy was still alive and well."

Locally, investigators had the drawing published in newspapers and magazines, put it on TV, passed it around hotels and bars frequented by a mostly homosexual clientele. They found no one who had seen the man.

Believing the victim had been a tourist, investigators checked with auto rental agencies in Broward in hopes of finding a report of an overdue car with the name of the murder victim on it. They visited local car towing agencies to check on abandoned vehicles that had been towed in the city after the murder. They found no clues.

"If he did rent a car, God knows where he rented it," said Mundy.

A month after the murder, the bloody palm print on the wall of the motel room led to the positive identification of Peter L. Ruggirello as a suspect. He was arrested in Jacksonville a year ago today. His accomplice, a man police identified as Wayne Moore, remains at large.

Mundy said Ruggirello never cooperated with investigators in providing the name of the murder victim. At his trial in Broward Circuit Court, Ruggirello said the man's name was Adam and that he had met him and Moore near the Backstreet bar on West Broward Boulevard near downtown. He denied being involved in the murder.

Prosecutor Peter LaPorte said an informant told authorities that Ruggirello once said the man's name was Henry Faulkner. Authorities aren't sure whether either of the names is the real one but believe Ruggirello knows more about the man he is convicted of killing than he has said.

"There are still a lot of questions that only Ruggirello

and the individual that is still at large could answer," said Mundy.

Because of those questions, Mundy keeps the investigation file on the top of his desk. The case is still open, though the chances of identifying the victim grow slimmer with time.

"My guess is he was from out of state," Mundy said. "He could have been reported missing in some other jurisdiction and we might never know it."

DOUBLE LIFE

MICHAEL BRYANT'S DOUBLE LIFE

Neighbors who knew the amiable man are shaken
by the murder charge against him.

LOS ANGELES TIMES
April 22, 1990

To THOSE WHO KNEW him in Woodland Hills,
Michael Bryant was a soft-spoken and generous man
who kept mostly to himself.

Though reclusive, he was far from unfriendly. He
was quick to volunteer his help to neighbors. He sent

Christmas cards and friendly notes to his landlady. He liked to show off the tricks he had taught his pet Doberman.

Bryant, 44, told people he was a freelance photographer. But often he spent his time gardening in his fenced backyard and was proud of the cherry tomatoes he gave to friends. "They were better than you could buy in a supermarket," his landlady said.

But authorities say Michael Bryant and the life he led in Los Angeles was a facade; that, in fact, Bryant was Francis W. Malinosky, a Vermont school administrator who dropped from sight in 1979 after he became the prime suspect in the disappearance of a teacher with whom he had been romantically involved.

Malinosky's double life came to an end earlier this month when he was traced by local and Vermont authorities to Woodland Hills. He was arrested and charged with the murder of the missing teacher. And while Malinosky waits in Los Angeles County jail for an extradition hearing, mystery still surrounds him.

Investigators say that when they searched Malinosky's belongings they found cameras and a business card suggesting he, indeed, was a photographer. But the only photos found were of him smiling amid fields of marijuana plants. No tomatoes were found at his house, but police said several pounds of packaged marijuana seeds were found in the garage. And in the unpretentious,

23-year-old Volkswagen he drove, investigators found a coffee can crammed with $217,000 in $100 bills.

"Finding this guy just opened up more questions," said Sgt. Leo Blais, a Vermont State Police detective who has tracked the Malinosky case for years. "I am trying to get an idea of what he has been doing for 10 years and it is hard. We don't know much about him."

Those who thought they knew Michael Bryant of Woodland Hills have also had to face the same enigma. A man they viewed as a good neighbor or tenant is charged with murder and is suspected of hiding behind at least four aliases and earning his living at least in part by selling marijuana seeds along with instructions on their planting and cultivation.

"This really comes out of left field," said Lilian Darling Holt, Bryant's landlord for nearly five years. "It is devastating. Michael was a marvelous tenant and person.

"This whole thing doesn't seem right," she said. "It seems that over the years there would have been something that would now click and I'd be able to say, 'Son of a gun, I now see how this could be.' But there is nothing like that. I just feel very bad. I wish I could do something for him."

Holt is not alone in being both perplexed and supportive of Bryant. Neighbors he was friendly with in the 4900 block of Topanga Canyon Boulevard have volunteered to care for his dog while he is in jail. And an attorney who met Bryant a few years ago in a coffee shop is now helping him fight extradition to Vermont.

"There is complete shock among those who knew him," said the attorney, Greff Michael Abrams. "He was the kind of guy most people would want as a neighbor."

Abrams said Malinosky disappeared from Vermont and began using false names because he was being hounded by authorities for a crime he did not commit.

"There is more to this case than meets the eye," Abrams said. "You don't need to be a genius to see why he would leave Vermont. He believed a witch hunt was under way, and he decided to leave."

But authorities insist they have made no mistake. Malinosky is the only suspect in the Nov. 5, 1979, disappearance and apparent murder of Judith Leo-Coneys. The 32-year-old mother of a small boy disappeared after telling friends she was going to a house owned by Malinosky.

"Everyone out here I talk to about him can't believe it," said Blais while he was in Los Angeles last week investigating Malinosky's life here. "They keep telling me he isn't the type."

So far Blais has established that Malinosky lived in the Los Angeles area in the early 1980s and worked as a house painter. He later moved to Utah and then back to Los Angeles, where beginning in late 1985 he lived alone in the two-bedroom Topanga Canyon Boulevard house.

Along the way, Malinosky somehow picked up one

alias — Barry Vandiver Bryant — that actually was the name of a real person, Blais said. The real Barry Bryant, of Charlotte, N.C., has since changed his name because of credit problems that began when Malinosky took his identity.

In 1979, Malinosky was, on the surface, an unlikely murder suspect. He had taught for several years in Burlington area schools and was known to many in the northern Vermont community. At 34, he was assistant director of special education for the Burlington School Department.

Bearded and slightly balding, he was a man who enjoyed the outdoors. He had an apartment in Burlington and owned a house in the rural town of Shelburne, which was more convenient for hunting and skiing. A mellow-voiced widower, his wife having shot herself to death in 1976, Malinosky was raising a daughter and son.

But in mid-1979 Malinosky's life apparently went into a tailspin when Leo-Coneys broke off a two-year relationship with him. According to Chittenden County court records, he was deeply hurt by the breakup, had sought psychiatric counseling and had been seen at least once spying through the windows of Leo-Coneys' apartment.

Two weeks before her disappearance, Leo-Coneys was held at gunpoint by Malinosky for several hours while he unsuccessfully attempted to persuade her to resume their relationship, records say.

On the morning of Nov. 5, 1979, Leo-Coneys told friends and relatives she was going to drop by Malinosky's home in Shelburne to retrieve something of hers. She chose that morning to go because she knew he was scheduled to be at work in Burlington.

But Leo-Coneys was never seen again. She was reported missing by her family later that day and investigators learned that Malinosky had not gone to work or even called his office to explain why. That night, when he was spotted driving his van in Shelburne and questioned by police, he said he took the day off to go bird hunting and did not see Leo-Coneys.

Leo-Coneys' car was found at a junkyard in the town of Roxbury the next day. A handwritten note on the windshield said the car could be stripped for parts and was signed "R. Peterson."

Malinosky was questioned repeatedly after the disappearance. But on Dec. 2, 1979, he put his children on a bus to his former in-laws' home, emptied his bank accounts and disappeared. Though Leo-Coneys' body has never been found, authorities claim they have amassed convincing evidence pointing to Malinosky.

According to court records, FBI experts matched Malinosky's handwriting to the note found on Leo-Coneys' car at the Roxbury junkyard. Investigators also found a cab driver who reported picking Malinosky up in Roxbury on the day of the woman's disappearance. A cab dispatcher who took the call remembered talking to Malinosky. She had once been one of his students.

Detectives had also noticed while interviewing Malinosky the first time that his parka was torn and leaking its down filling. The same type of down was found in Leo-Coneys' car, court records say.

Police believed after Malinosky's disappearance that he might have killed himself, and the case languished without any charges being filed.

In 1986, the Leo-Coneys case was assigned to Blais to be updated and, using a computer search, the detective learned Malinosky was alive and had apparently lived in Salt Lake City in the mid-1980s, where he used his own name to get a driver's license.

Blais went to Utah but Malinosky was gone.

Once again, the case languished, until last year when a new state attorney, William Sorrell, was appointed and made the Leo-Coneys investigation a priority. The case was presented Feb. 20, 1990, to a grand jury, which concluded that Leo-Coneys was dead, and a warrant was issued two days later charging Malinosky with her slaying.

According to court records, Malinosky's daughter told investigators she had met her father earlier this year at the St. Moritz Hotel in New York City. Blais learned that the hotel room Malinosky used was paid for by a credit card issued to a Barry Vandiver Bryant. From that point, credit card billings under that name were traced to four private mailboxes in the San Fernando Valley and Hollywood.

Members of the Los Angeles Police Department fugitive squad questioned the private mailbox proprietors, who identified Barry Bryant as Malinosky. And on April 12, the detectives were alerted by one of the mail-drop operators that Bryant had just picked up his mail.

Police and FBI agents immediately went to the area on Ventura Boulevard in Woodland Hills, but Bryant was already gone.

The investigators decided to check area motels, and a clerk at a Best Western in the 21800 block of Ventura Boulevard identified a photo of Malinosky as a guest who had been renting a room since Feb. 20 — the day the grand jury hearing began in Vermont. Investigators now believe he moved to the motel after learning, possibly through friends or family in Vermont, that the grand jury was investigating the case.

Police watched the motel room and Malinosky was arrested that afternoon when he drove up in his 1967 Volkswagen. He had papers identifying himself as Michael Bryant and that showed his address as a house about five blocks away on Topanga Canyon Boulevard.

In the car, police found the coffee can containing $217,000, along with a material normally used to keep moisture out of packages. Detectives said the powder indicated the can of money may have been buried previously.

Investigators were puzzled by where Malinosky had gotten the cash. But the next day, his house was searched and dozens of packets of marijuana seeds were found in the garage. Police theorized that Malinosky may have accumulated the cache of money by selling drugs or the seeds.

Los Angeles Police Detective Ronald Tuckett said marijuana cultivation instructions and other drug paraphernalia were found in the garage.

"It looks like he may have been in the mail-order business," Tuckett said.

Though the drug investigation is continuing, it is unlikely local charges will be filed against Malinosky because they could hinder his extradition to Vermont to face the murder charge, authorities said.

Alerted on the morning of April 12, the day Malinosky picked up his mail, Blais was already flying from Vermont to Los Angeles when the man he had pursued since 1986 was taken into custody. The detective and suspect met for the first time in a holding cell.

"All he did was stare at the ground," Blais said. "He was very upset. I introduced myself and he said, 'I know who you are.' I said, 'I know who you are, too, but do you want me to call you Frank or Michael or Barry or what?' He said to call him Frank. It was a strange feeling to finally meet him face to face."

DEATH OF AN HEIRESS

MURDER OF KANAN HEIR
REMAINS A MYSTERY

Judy Kanan, a tough-minded businesswoman, came from a pioneer family. Two men are still suspects in the 1985 slaying, but a detective says he has no idea who killed her.

LOS ANGELES TIMES
January 29, 1990

F IVE YEARS AGO TODAY, Judy Kanan, a strong-willed 68-year-old businesswoman and descendant of a pioneer family, stopped by a Woodland Hills corral to feed her pets — six Arabian horses that she fawned over like children.

It was her daily ritual to care for the horses she loved, and residents near the stables on a cul-de-sac on Collins Street knew the sight of Kanan and her old Chevy well.

But on that Tuesday afternoon — Jan. 29, 1985 — a killer also knew Kanan's routine well. When she got out of her car, a masked gunman stepped forward and shot her four times. She died on the sidewalk next to the corral.

One of the detectives originally assigned to the murder, Phil Quartararo, remains on the case. Recently, as he looked through one of the thick files he has filled with investigative reports over the years, he offered a quick summary of the case.

"I don't have any idea who killed Judy Kanan," he said.

That is how things stand with the murder that gripped public attention for weeks after it occurred. It is now largely forgotten — except by those who knew Judy Kanan well or have the responsibility of looking for her killer.

The case remains a puzzle for Los Angeles police and a source of bitter frustration for those who wait for justice for Kanan.

"We don't want what happened to be forgotten," the victim's niece and family spokeswoman, Patty Kanan, said last week. "If people don't remember it, it will go away. We don't want that because we want to catch this person.

"The killer is still out there. That's the frightening part. Anyone who would kill an old woman would kill anybody. That should scare everybody, not just us."

Judy Kanan was a descendant of the Waring family, which settled Agoura in the 1860s. By the 1980s, Kanan and her older sister, Patricia Kanan, had parlayed inheritances and acquisitions into landholdings in Agoura worth millions of dollars. Kanan Road, which runs north-south through Agoura, was named for the family.

The sisters lived together in Hollywood and at the time of the murder owned and operated Kanan Village Shopping Center — the centerpiece of the family's holdings — in Agoura. In the shopping center, the sisters also operated a small restaurant specializing in roast rabbit and chicken.

Judy Kanan was an enigma. Of the two sisters she was the one on the front line of their business deals. She forged a reputation as a tough-minded, aggressive businesswoman who often took disputes to court — once she even settled a business argument on the syndicated *People's Court* television show. At the shopping center, she was known to tenaciously press workers to finish projects or tenants to pay rent.

Yet friends and other business associates described her as kind and fiercely loyal. Despite her family's wealth, she worked many hours each day at the shopping center and restaurant. She drove a 13-year-old car and lived modestly. And she took time out each afternoon to drive from the shopping center to Woodland Hills to feed and care for her horses.

But police said it was her tough business style and litigious image that left her with many enemies and perhaps provided a motive for her slaying. After she was killed, one Agoura businessman said, "You're going to have half the population of Agoura as suspects."

Quartararo said the killing was carefully planned and executed. The killer knew her routine and knew she would be alone when she fed her horses each afternoon.

"Whoever it was, he chose the one time Judy and my mother were separated," Patty Kanan said. "It was the only place he could get to her."

The man who gunned Kanan down was wearing a raincoat and had a mask or hood to disguise himself, according to a lone witness to the slaying. The car in which he fled had been stolen from a car dealer's lot. Twenty minutes after the killing it was parked near Ventura Boulevard and set on fire. That obliterated any evidence and helped cover the killer's trail.

The killing had many of the earmarks of a professional assassination but police still can't say for sure that it was.

"There was almost no physical evidence for us to work with," Quartararo said.

Detectives investigated Kanan's business deals and disputes. They examined each lawsuit, every complaint

Kanan had made to friends or authorities and interviewed dozens of people.

In the weeks after the slaying two men emerged as "prime" suspects because of disputes they had had with Kanan, Quartararo said.

The first man had argued with Kanan at the shopping center a week before the killing. The dispute centered on the man's desire to rent space in the shopping center for a stereo equipment store. The two quarreled over the rent and then Kanan refused to rent to the man at all.

During the following weekend Kanan received several threatening phone calls from an unidentified woman. The following Tuesday she was killed.

After police publicized a composite drawing of the unidentified man, he came forward with an attorney but refused to answer questions about the slaying. His identity was not released.

Detectives determined that the man's girlfriend had made the threatening phone calls to Kanan and a warrant was obtained to search the man's home. But no evidence was found connecting the man to the murder, Quartararo said. He was not arrested.

The second man, whom police also declined to identify, had been accused by Kanan several weeks before the slaying of stealing building supplies from the shopping center. Quartararo said the man was arrested in the theft but denied stealing anything. A week before the killing, authorities dropped charges against him.

Quartararo said detectives believed that the second suspect might have held a grudge against Kanan. A warrant was obtained from a judge and the man's home was searched, but again there was no evidence linked to Kanan's death and no arrest was made.

Both search warrants remain under court seal, and other details of the investigation of the two men were unavailable. Quartararo said no evidence was found linking the men to the slaying, but neither has been eliminated as a suspect.

Quartararo, who routinely handles other murder cases in the west San Fernando Valley, said it has been three years since a new lead has come in on the Kanan case. He believes it will take more than detective work to break the case.

"If we don't have anybody come forward with some information, we aren't going to solve this one," Quartararo said.

That the case remains unsolved is frustrating to Kanan's family. Patricia Kanan, now in her late 70s, sold the restaurant she operated with her sister. Because of ill health, she turned management of the shopping center over to her daughter, Patty.

The older Kanan declined to comment on the case.

"Frustration is the word for what we feel," Patty Kanan said. "And we feel sadness. We really want to know who did this."

Patricia Kanan, who is unmarried, moved last year

from the home she had shared with her sister and now lives with her daughter in an undisclosed location. Though the Kanans do not live in fear of the killer, they anxiously wait for justice.

"My mother and our family have the basic concern that someone out there has killed someone and believes they have gotten away with it," Patty Kanan said. "It could be anybody. It was a chilling and very calculated act. And that person is still out there. I hate the thought of someone getting away with murder."

NEPHEW IDENTIFIED AS SOLE SUSPECT IN KANAN KILLING

September 29, 1990

Nearly six years after Judy Kanan, a strong-willed businesswoman and descendant of a pioneer family, was shot to death at a Woodland Hills horse stable, the investigation of the unsolved slaying has narrowed to one person — her nephew, according to police and court documents.

A search warrant filed this month in Van Nuys Municipal Court identifies 34-year-old Michael Kanan, the son of the victim's brother, as the killer.

After the slaying, according to the court document, the suspect told an acquaintance who later became a police informant: "It's a real trip to see something you're responsible for. . . . The bitch got what she deserved."

Los Angeles police say they are seeking additional evidence before asking the Los Angeles County district attorney's office to file murder charges against Michael Kanan, who is in jail on an unrelated burglary charge.

The suspect, through his attorney, denied having any part in the slaying.

Judy Kanan, 68, was shot four times by a masked gunman in a raincoat on Jan. 29, 1985, as she followed her daily routine and arrived at a stable at the end of a cul-de-sac on Collins Street. She was there to feed six Arabian horses she owned. The killer gunned her down on the sidewalk and escaped in a stolen car that was later abandoned and set on fire.

Police said little evidence was left behind at the shooting scene. And while the investigation stalled, the mystery of who killed Judy Kanan deepened.

The victim was a descendant of the Waring family, which settled Agoura in the 1860s. By the 1980s, Judy Kanan and her older sister, Patricia Kanan, had parlayed inheritances and acquisitions into landholdings in Agoura worth millions of dollars.

When she was gunned down, police acknowledged there was no shortage of potential suspects and concentrated largely on reviewing her business disputes. The killing prompted one Agoura businessman who was interviewed at the time to say: "You're going to have half the population of Agoura as suspects. The most hated woman in Agoura got assassinated."

In January of this year, as the fifth anniversary of the killing approached, police said they still were no closer to solving the mystery. "I don't have any idea who killed Judy Kanan," Detective Phil Quartararo said at the time.

Court records and police, however, reveal that investigators now believe the slaying was carried out by Michael Kanan and motivated by a financial dispute within the family.

Shortly after the fifth anniversary of Judy Kanan's death, a person who knows Michael Kanan came forward with details about the slaying. That person said he had been asked by the suspect to kill Judy Kanan.

According to court records, the informant told police the slaying centered on a dispute between Judy Kanan and her brother, George Richard Kanan — Michael Kanan's father — over a $2,600 loan. Coupled with that was the belief George Kanan impressed upon his son that Judy Kanan had unfairly controlled most of the family's land, the informant said.

"The informant indicated that George Richard Kanan hated his sister and preached this hatred to his son, Michael . . . ," the search warrant reads in part. "George Kanan had preached to his son that Judy Kanan had stolen all of his property."

According to the court records, the informant said the slaying unfolded this way:

In 1984, George Kanan signed an agreement to borrow $2,600 from his sister for unknown reasons. But by the end of the year, he believed he was going to default on the loan and thereby lose a large piece of property he owned in Agoura to her.

"The informant stated that George Kanan was extremely upset Judy Kanan made him sign the agreement," according to the search warrant.

"Shortly after the loan was made, Michael Kanan approached the informant with a plan to kill Judy Kanan. . . . Michael Kanan had originally planned to kill both Judy and her sister, Pat, at their Agoura restaurant and had planned to make it look like a robbery. The plan was later changed to kill only Judy and it was to be done at the corrals where she went daily to feed her horses," the warrant stated.

The informant said that a few weeks before the killing, Michael Kanan showed him a handgun that would be used to kill Judy Kanan. Police and the informant believe the gun was stolen during a burglary of a car parked near Balboa Park in the Sepulveda Dam Recreation Area. But neither the gun nor its owner has been found.

The informant told police that in mid-January 1985 he stole a car and parked it near the stable where Judy Kanan's horses were kept. The car was to be used as a getaway car after the killing, but the car was noticed by police Jan. 25 and impounded.

The informant said he believed the plan would not go any further, but four days later he said he was shocked when he saw a news report on television about the slaying of Judy Kanan.

"...it was done in the same manner as previously planned," the search warrant reads. "Shortly after watching the newscast, the informant confronted Michael Kanan, who admitted to him that he had committed the murder.... The informant believes that Michael Kanan committed the murder because he sensed that the informant would not be able to go through with the plan."

Quartararo, who has been assigned to the case since its start, said Michael Kanan was questioned along with other family members in the early stages of the case, but "we never narrowed in on him."

About a year after the slaying, Michael Kanan became a fugitive when he jumped bail after his arrest for a commercial burglary in Van Nuys, police said. He wasn't arrested until last month in Burbank and now is being held in the county jail without bail.

William H. Schultz, an attorney representing Michael Kanan, denied that his client had any involvement in the Kanan slaying.

"The charges are groundless and illogical," Schultz said. He declined further comment.

George Richard Kanan could not be located for comment.

Police are confident of the informant's story because he has furnished details about the crime that were never made public. They declined to identify him as a safety precaution.

Acting on the informant's story, police earlier this month searched a rental storage unit in Chatsworth used by Michael Kanan. A raincoat and gloves were found, but detectives did not find the gun.

Meantime, Quartararo said he has corroborated some of the informant's story, finding legal documents relating to the $2,600 loan and confirming that a stolen car was impounded by police on the Collins Street cul-de-sac four days before Judy Kanan was shot there.

Before seeking charges against the suspect, police said they must also corroborate the informant's version of where the gun used in the slaying came from. Because Michael Kanan was once arrested for attempting to burglarize a car near the Balboa Golf Course in the Sepulveda Dam Recreation Area, police believe the weapon might have come from a similar burglary in that area.

Quartararo said he has been searching through reports on crimes in the sprawling park area for the months prior to the killing but has not found a report containing a stolen gun. He asked that anyone who might have had a handgun stolen while in the park area in late 1984 or early 1985 contact police. He cited a $50,000 reward for information leading to a conviction in the Kanan slaying.

"We do need to corroborate this part of the story," Quartararo said. "If we can establish that the gun came from a car in that area as the informant said, the district

attorney's office will file the case" without having the actual weapon used in the slaying in evidence.

CHARGES WILL NOT BE
FILED IN KANAN CASE

March 21, 1991

Prosecutors have decided not to file charges against a man
suspected in the highly publicized slaying six years ago of
his aunt, a wealthy landowner and descendant of a pioneer Agoura family. However, Los Angeles police continue to identify him as the prime suspect.

After a lengthy review by the Los Angeles County district attorney's office, prosecutors decided there was insufficient evidence to charge Michael Kanan, 34, with
the murder of Judy Kanan, said Sandi Gibbons, spokeswoman for the prosecutors' office.

Michael Kanan, through his attorney, has in the past
denied any part in the killing.

Judy Kanan, 68, a descendant of the family that settled
Agoura in the 1860s, was shot four times by a masked
gunman in a raincoat who approached her as she arrived
at a Woodland Hills stable on Jan. 29, 1985, to feed horses
she kept there.

The killer escaped and no arrests were made. Early
last year, an informant who said he was troubled by feelings of guilt contacted police and identified Michael
Kanan, son of the victim's brother, as the gunman.

According to court records, the informant said the slaying was motivated by long-simmering family tensions brought to a head by a dispute over a $2,600 loan from Judy Kanan to Michael Kanan's father, George Richard Kanan.

Detectives felt no need to arrest Michael Kanan because he was already in jail for violating probation terms on an unrelated burglary conviction. He is now serving a two-year prison term for the probation violation.

After corroborating parts of the informant's story of how the murder took place, detectives seeking a murder charge submitted the case to the district attorney late last year.

Gibbons declined to reveal why the case was rejected, saying the investigation is continuing.

The investigators on the case did not dispute the district attorney's decision not to file charges.

"It was a close call," Lt. William Gaida said, and Michael Kanan "remains the primary suspect. We need to get additional information or evidence. We consider the informant to be reliable and we are convinced we are looking in the right direction."

According to court records filed during the investigation, Michael Kanan had once asked the informant to help him kill Judy Kanan, suggesting a plan that was similar to the way the actual killing occurred.

The informant, according to the court records, said the slaying was later carried out without his involvement, and afterward Michael Kanan told him, "It's a real trip to see something you are responsible for. . . . The bitch got what she deserved."

The informant also told investigators of a storage locker Michael Kanan used where police then seized a raincoat and gloves officers believe were worn during the killing.

However, police conceded that the informant's credibility could be questioned by a jury if the case were brought to trial now because some of the details of the crime he gave police could not be corroborated by investigators.

The gun used in the slaying has never been found. A key part of the informant's story was that Michael Kanan stole the gun from a car parked by a jogger in the Sepulveda Dam Recreation Area, said Detective Phil Quartararo.

Quartararo reviewed reports of hundreds of crimes in that area in the months before the killing without discovering one involving such a theft, he said.

Quartararo, who has been assigned to the killing from the beginning, said he has no plans to drop the case, but the investigation has gone "as far as we may be able to go unless somebody else comes forward."

NOTE: Five years after prosecutors decided not to file charges against Michael Kanan, he engaged police in an armed standoff at his mother's San Fernando Valley home. He shot and killed a dog and a horse and then fired several shots at arriving police officers. No officers were injured. After a two-hour standoff, Kanan killed himself by shooting himself in the head. He died without ever admitting he had been Judy Kanan's killer. Police later revealed that the informant who in 1990 pointed the finger at Michael Kanan in his aunt's death had been his own brother.

HOLLYWOOD HOMICIDE

'COTTON CLUB' CASE LED TO ARREST IN '84 SLAYING OF PROSTITUTE

LOS ANGELES TIMES

June 25, 1989

FIVE YEARS AGO, June Mincher, a 245-pound prostitute with a lavender Rolls-Royce, was shot to death on a Van Nuys sidewalk by a swift and efficient killer, setting off an investigation that unearthed a bizarre cast of characters and seamy tales, but convicted no one.

This month some of the mystery appears to be unraveling in a court hearing into another killing a world away — the world of the "Cotton Club" slaying with its Hollywood celebrities and high-finance film and cocaine deals.

Testimony in the Cotton Club hearing, and related documents filed with the court, contain accusations that both slayings were carried out by some of the same hired killers, who boasted of their work to an informant wearing a tape recorder for investigators.

The question of who might have hired them to kill Mincher is still open, but at least one document filed with the court quotes an informant as saying that it was the grandmother of the man who had been acquitted of the killing. An attorney for the woman, a Beverly Hills investment executive, denied the accusation. Police say they are still investigating and will not comment.

Mincher, who billed herself in local sex-oriented publications as a "Sexy Black & Indian Goddess" with a 56-inch bust, was shot to death May 3, 1984. Two years later, Gregory Alan Cavalli, a 24-year-old body builder from a prominent Beverly Hills family, was charged with her murder. Authorities said he drove the getaway car after a hit man killed Mincher.

But at Cavalli's trial, prosecutors could not produce or even name the hit man. And the chief witnesses against Cavalli included a former cocaine addict, a transsexual performer in pornographic films and a woman recovering from a nervous breakdown suffered after her son killed her mother.

Fast Vote for Acquittal

At the end of a three-week trial in 1986, Cavalli walked out of the Van Nuys Courthouse a free man. It took a jury less than an hour to find him not guilty.

But now, three years later, the Mincher murder case begins a new chapter.

Authorities have charged two men with killing Mincher, identifying them as bodyguards who formerly worked for a security firm that the Cavalli family had hired. Detectives now say Cavalli was not the getaway driver and was not even present the night of the killing.

The question of who ordered Mincher's killing remains, but authorities say Cavalli is not a target of the investigation because he can't be tried for the same crime twice.

"Never," said Los Angeles Police Sgt. Ed Entwisle. "He has been tried and that is it."

Investigators will not discuss whom they consider suspects. But in a summary of the investigation filed with Los Angeles Superior Court, in connection with the Cotton Club case, the key informant in the case is quoted as telling officers that one of the suspects told him that Mincher "had been bothering a wealthy Italian family and the grandmother contracted the 'hit.'"

Attorney Mitchell W. Egers, who represents the Cavalli family, identified "grandmother" as a reference to Mary Bowles, a partner in the Beverly Hills real-estate investment firm of Bowles & Associates. "There is no other grandmother . . . with a part in this case," he said, denying that anyone in the family had anything to do with the Mincher killing.

"It's absurd, it's crazy, it's absolutely impossible," Egers said. "It is beyond my conception that anybody in the Cavalli family would have anything to do with anything illegal, let alone a murder. They are gentle, refined people with an excellent reputation."

New Leads Uncovered

New leads in the Mincher case emerged almost by accident in the last two years during the lengthy Los Angeles County Sheriff's Department investigation of the slaying of would-be movie producer Roy Radin.

William Molony Mentzer, 39, of Canoga Park and Robert Ulmer Lowe, 42, of Rockville, Md., two of the alleged hit men arrested in Radin's 1983 slaying, have also been charged with killing Mincher in 1984.

Mentzer has pleaded not guilty, and Lowe is fighting extradition from Maryland.

A preliminary hearing is under way in Los Angeles Superior Court into the slaying of Radin, which was dubbed the Cotton Club case because Radin was killed during a financial dispute over the making of the movie of that name.

Although the Mincher murder is involved in the hearing, it has been overshadowed by the headline-grabbing testimony in the Radin killing, which has involved cocaine deals, limousines and accusations involving movie producer Robert Evans.

But investigative records filed with the court and the statements of prosecutors and detectives about the Mincher case weave a portrait of an investigation that was started and stopped two different times before the present inquiry began.

According to stories told by friends and associates at the time of her death, June Mincher, 29, parlayed advertisements in underground newspapers offering sexual services into a lucrative lifestyle. Friends told investigators that she had spent at least $20,000 on cosmetic surgery to alter her face and hips and enlarge her bust. She drove a lavender Rolls-Royce and carried as much as $12,000 in a case beneath her wig.

In the summer of 1983, according to testimony at Cavalli's trial, Cavalli began calling Mincher after seeing her ad in an underground newspaper. The telephone relationship lasted several months, with the two talking for several hours on some days. Cavalli wanted to meet Mincher but she declined. Finally, he went to her West Hollywood apartment and broke down the door.

Cavalli discovered that Mincher weighed 60 or 70

pounds more than she appeared to in the picture in her advertisement, and he ended the relationship.

Angered by the rejection, Mincher then began to harass Cavalli; his father, Richard Cavalli; and other relatives, including Bowles, with repeated threatening phone calls. Mincher was suspected by authorities of firebombing Greg Cavalli's car in late 1983 and setting fire to his father's military-surplus store in Santa Monica in 1984.

The Cavalli family spent $200,000 on private security guards to protect them from Mincher, according to trial testimony, and Gregory Cavalli moved to Phoenix to get away from her.

On May 3, 1984, Mincher had just left an apartment in the 6800 block of Sepulveda Boulevard with a friend when she was shot seven times in the head. She died instantly. The friend was shot in the chest but survived. The gunman ran to a waiting car, which sped away.

Los Angeles police began investigating Cavalli's possible involvement in the slaying within three hours of the shooting, according to court records. Though two witnesses identified Cavalli as the driver of the getaway car, investigators could not identify the gunman. The investigation stalled and was shelved two months later.

As is routine with unsolved killings, the case was reopened by two new investigators the following year. According to police records, they immediately focused on the more than six bodyguards who had been provided to the Cavalli family by a Studio City firm, A. Michael Pascal & Associates. The detectives got the names but could not locate and interview all of the men because they had left Pascal.

"At that particular time, we were trying to get all the bodyguards identified," Entwisle said recently. "We were never able to determine if these were the suspects in the killing although our investigation pointed that way."

Went Ahead with Trial

Two of the bodyguards they could not find were Lowe and Mentzer. In December 1985 police and prosecutors decided to go ahead with the arrest and trial of Cavalli without knowing who the hit man was.

During the trial in June 1986 a transsexual pornographic film performer who was a close friend of Mincher's testified about the relationship between Cavalli and Mincher. But the case relied most heavily on the two witnesses who had identified Cavalli as the getaway driver.

However, on the stand, one of those witnesses admitted that at the time of the shooting, he was a cocaine addict and could have made a mistake. The other witness, Cavalli's attorneys brought out, had originally told police that he could not see the driver.

Jurors later said the witnesses lacked credibility and chose to believe the defense's contention that Cavalli was in Phoenix, and had made phone calls from there, when the killing took place. Cavalli was acquitted, and the Mincher case was shelved once again.

Meanwhile, sheriff's investigators working on the Radin killing of 1983 were investigating Mentzer and Lowe.

Radin, 33, of Long Island, disappeared May 13, 1983, after getting into a limousine in Hollywood to go to a dinner engagement to discuss the financial backing for *Cotton Club*. His decomposed body was found a month later on a wilderness shooting range south of Gorman.

Mentzer and Lowe were among the possible suspects identified in the slaying, but the sheriff's investigation moved slowly until 1987 when deputies contacted William Rider, a former security chief for *Hustler* magazine publisher Larry Flynt. Rider knew Mentzer and Lowe from security jobs.

Slaying Described

Rider, according to court records and testimony in the Cotton Club case, told investigators that Mentzer and Lowe had told him about murders they had been involved in. One was the Radin killing. Another was the slaying of a woman in Van Nuys who the men apparently thought was a transvestite.

Rider told the investigators of a 1986 conversation he had with Lowe while they were on a security job in Texas.

"Lowe began drinking heavily and told Mr. Rider about Mentzer murdering a black transvestite," a sheriff's investigative report says, and continued:

"Lowe said that he drove the getaway vehicle and that Mentzer shot the victim several times while standing on Sepulveda Boulevard in the San Fernando Valley.... Mentzer also shot the victim's companion, but the companion survived.

"Lowe stated Mentzer began calling the murdered victim names and kicking her after the shooting, and Lowe, who was in the driver's seat of their vehicle, had to call to Mentzer to get in the car so they could get away before the police arrived."

Gun Matched to Slugs

The investigators connected the facts Rider gave to the Mincher slaying. Rider later told investigators that he had unknowingly lent Mentzer the gun used in the killing and turned over a .22-caliber semiautomatic pistol, equipped with a silencer. According to the court records, investigators matched the gun to the slugs that killed Mincher.

Rider next went undercover for the sheriff's investigators, agreeing to meet with Lowe, Mentzer and a third former bodyguard for the Pascal firm, Robert Leroy Deremer, 38, while the conversations were secretly tape-recorded.

In May 1988 while sitting with Rider in a car in
Frederick, Md., according to sheriff's records, Deremer
spoke about the Mincher killing and said he drove
Mentzer by the murder scene shortly after the shooting
so that Mentzer could see what police were doing. The
next day, Rider met with Lowe at a bar in the same city
and while the conversation was secretly recorded, Lowe
told of his part in the killing, the records say.

Two months later, it was Mentzer's turn. Rider met
him in Los Angeles and steered the tape-recorded conversation toward the murder. According to the records,
Mentzer said that in the weeks before the murder, he had
placed a bomb under Mincher's car but it failed to go off.
He said he had also broken into Mincher's apartment
and pistol-whipped her. In another conversation,
Mentzer said he used hollow-point bullets during the
killing because he believed — erroneously — that they
were impossible to match to a weapon.

The tapes of the conversations, along with testimony
by Rider, are expected to be key evidence against
Mentzer and Lowe, if they come to trial. Authorities said
last week that Deremer has agreed to testify against his
two fellow bodyguards and will not be charged in the
case.

While authorities are confident that they finally know
how Mincher was killed, the question of who ordered
her death remains unclear.

3rd Look into Case

Earlier this year, Los Angeles police began their third look at the case after the sheriff's investigation broke it open.

"We're following up on loose ends," Entwisle said. "There are still people out there that were involved."

Authorities declined to comment on who the suspects are. But one thing they are sure of is that Gregory Cavalli cannot be tried again.

"As far as Mr. Cavalli is concerned, the case is over," said Deputy Dist. Atty. Andrew W. Diamond, who headed the unsuccessful prosecution in 1986. "He can't ever be prosecuted again for killing June Mincher."

Deputy Dist. Atty. David P. Conn, who is handling the case against Mentzer and Lowe, would not comment. "I don't want to speculate on Gregory Cavalli's role," Conn said. "He has been acquitted."

Cavalli, who has moved back to Southern California since his trial, could not be reached for comment.

Pascal, whose security firm is now in Beverly Hills, confirmed last week that Mentzer and Lowe worked for his firm when it was hired by the Cavalli family. But he would not comment further. Pascal has not been charged with any crime.

THE FAMILY

4 MEN ARRESTED IN LAKE VIEW TERRACE QUADRUPLE KILLING

LOS ANGELES TIMES

September 30, 1988

FOUR MEN WERE ARRESTED Thursday in a quadruple slaying in which two men, a mother and her 28-month-old daughter were shot to death at a Lake View Terrace house where "rock" cocaine was sold, Los Angeles police said.

293

The four men may also be implicated in two more San Fernando Valley murders, police said.

A team of nearly 200 police officers, including members of the department's Special Weapons and Tactics team, raided three fortified drug houses and 12 other locations in the northeast Valley before all the suspects were arrested, a department spokesman said.

Lt. Fred Nixon identified the suspects as Stanley Bryant, 30, of Pacoima; Antonio Johnson, 28, of Lake View Terrace; Nash Newbil, 52, of Lake View Terrace; and Levi Flack Jr., 24, whose address had not been determined.

Held without Bail

Bryant and Johnson were arrested on suspicion of murder, and Newbil and Flack were arrested on suspicion of being accessories to murder. All four were being held without bail at the Foothill Division jail.

"The arrests of all four of these people refer to the quadruple murder," Nixon said. "There are indications they are implicated in two others. The warrants for the searches of the 15 locations came out of the investigation of all six murders. The investigation is continuing."

The locations of the raids and arrests, as well as complete details of the investigation, were unavailable Thursday. But detectives said the arrests stemmed from an investigation centered on the Lake View Terrace shooting Aug. 28 that left the four people dead.

In that incident, police said, two St. Louis men, Andre Armstrong, 31, and James Brown, 43, were killed after they went inside the house in the 11400 block of Wheeler Avenue. After the two were shot, a man ran out with a shotgun and fired into the car in which Armstrong and Brown had traveled to the house.

The blasts killed Lorretha Anderson English, 23, of Seaside and her daughter, Chemise, who were sitting in the backseat. English's 1-year-old son, who was also in the backseat, was only slightly injured. Police would not release the boy's name.

After the shooting, police said, the man with the shotgun jumped into the car and drove about a mile away from the house before abandoning it in an alley. The bodies and the injured child were still inside.

Meanwhile, the bodies of Armstrong and Brown were loaded in another car and driven away from the house, police said. Police found them three days later in Lopez Canyon.

No Comment

Nixon said he could not comment on the motive for the slayings. Earlier, police speculated that a drug dispute ignited the violence.

County records show that Newbil is the owner of the Wheeler Avenue house, which police said had been the scene of drug sales for two to three months before the shootings.

The house was formerly owned by Jeffrey A. Bryant, 37, once described by police as a drug kingpin who controlled a sales network in the northeast Valley.

In February 1986 Jeffrey Bryant pleaded guilty to operating a drug house at the Wheeler Avenue location and was sentenced to four years in state prison. He is believed to be the brother of Stanley Bryant, one of the suspects arrested Thursday.

Possible Link

The Wheeler Avenue case may be linked to shootings July 31, in which Douglas Henegan, 21, of Panorama City was killed, and Sunday, in which Tracy Anderson, 24, of Sylmar was slain, police said. The victims of those shootings were close friends, police said.

Henegan was gunned down while he sat with friends on a curb at Hansen Dam Park. Anderson was shot to death on a Pacoima street after an argument involving several men. On Monday, Leroy Wheeler, 19, of Sylmar surrendered to police and was arrested on suspicion of murder in the Anderson case.

Police declined to discuss the motives for the Henegan and Anderson killings or how they may relate to the other four. However, Nixon said Wheeler is also suspected of involvement in the quadruple slaying.

DRUG RING KINGPIN CALLS THE SHOTS FROM PRISON, POLICE SAY

October 16, 1988

Los Angeles police think that a prison inmate in San Diego is directing a San Fernando Valley drug organization whose top members were charged this month in the slayings of four people at a Lake View Terrace "rock" house.

Investigators said they think that the inmate, Jeffrey A. Bryant, 37, of Pacoima, is the leader of a drug ring with as many as 200 members that has controlled the sale of rock cocaine in the northeast Valley for nearly a decade.

Bryant is serving a four-year sentence at the Richard S. Donovan Correctional Facility for a 1986 conviction for operating a drug house.

"We believe he calls the shots from prison," said Lt. Bernard D. Conine, chief of Foothill Division detectives.

Linked to Statewide Gang

Authorities said Bryant and other top-level members of his organization have been linked to the Black Guerrilla Family, a gang formed in California prisons in the early

1970s. The BGF, as it is more commonly known, at first focused on revolutionary politics but now is accused of operating a statewide drug network, authorities said.

Bryant faces no charges in the Aug. 28 quadruple slaying at the house he previously owned in the 11400 block of Wheeler Avenue. But investigators said the arrests of several lieutenants in the killings have depleted his organization's top echelon.

Although police think they eventually will be able to break up the Valley organization, they noted that lower-level members are in line to take over for those arrested in the Wheeler Avenue killings.

"We know there are people in the organization who want to step up," Conine said. "The bottom line is, you can still buy rock cocaine in Pacoima."

Through informants and witnesses and from evidence gathered during searches of 26 locations where organization members lived and operated, authorities said, they have pieced together what happened at the house on Wheeler Avenue and why.

Andre Louis Armstrong, 31, and James Brown, 43, both of the Pacoima area, were hit with shotgun blasts at the door of the house, police said.

They said Lorretha Anderson English, 23, of Seaside, and her 28-month-old daughter, Chemise, were fatally shot while waiting in a car parked out front. English's 1½-year-old son, Carlos, was slightly injured by flying glass.

So far, 11 people, including Bryant's younger brother,

Stanley Bryant, 30, have been charged in the killings. Stanley Bryant; Le Roy Wheeler, 19; Levie Slack III, 24; Tannis Bryant Curry, 26; James Franklin Williams III, 19; John Preston Settle, 28; and Antonio Arceneaux, whose age was unavailable, each face four charges of murder and one charge of attempted murder. All are Pacoima residents.

Antonio Johnson, 28, and Nash Newbil, 52, both of Lake View Terrace, and William Gene Settle, 30, and Provine McCloria, 19, both of Pacoima, each face charges of accessory to murder.

The Settle brothers, McCloria and Arceneaux are still sought.

Only Stanley Bryant, Wheeler, Slack and Johnson have been arraigned. Each pleaded not guilty. Wheeler also has pleaded not guilty to a fifth murder, the Sept. 25 fatal shooting of a Pacoima drug dealer who police think was attempting to compete with the Bryant Organization.

According to police and court records, the slayings occurred during a power struggle in which Armstrong, who had served a prison term for a killing attributed to the organization, demanded money and a top position in the so-called Bryant Organization.

A Group Decision

Instead of giving Armstrong what he wanted, the organization decided to kill him at a meeting at the Lake View

Terrace house, where the group kept money and cocaine, authorities said. When other people showed up with Armstrong, gang members decided to eliminate them too, police said.

Wheeler told a police informant, "They had to be killed to protect the organization," according to court records.

"They were shot . . . through the metal door," he is quoted as saying, referring to Armstrong and Brown. "The woman and baby had to be killed. She was writing down license numbers. I had to shoot them."

Authorities think the Bryant Organization took control of cocaine sales in the northeast Valley after James H. (Doc) Holiday, a leader of the BGF, was accused in a 1979 double murder in Pacoima.

The charges against Holiday, who police think had controlled cocaine traffic in the area, were dismissed. But he was convicted of the attempted murder of a witness in the case and was sent to prison, leaving the northeast Valley to Jeffrey Bryant's group, authorities said.

The Bryant Organization began to distribute cocaine through street sales and at as many as six drug houses in the Pacoima and Lake View Terrace areas, police said. The organization soon earned a reputation for violence, police said.

"The rock cocaine business is controlled by Jeff Bryant," according to a police statement filed in the 1986 drug case that sent Bryant to prison. In the words of the statement, "He is the head of an organization consisting of family members and associates, which exists for the sole purpose of the distribution and selling of large quantities of cocaine."

Police think the organization was responsible for several unsolved slayings and attempted murders. Another court document filed in the 1986 case says an informant told police: "Jeff Bryant is a sergeant-at-arms in the BGF and often uses BGF soldiers to commit shootings and murders to enforce his hold on the cocaine distribution in the Pacoima area."

Chance to Network

Bryant served time in prison in the mid-1970s for a bank-robbery conviction and may have become associated with the BGF then, police said. "Our intelligence shows the Bryant Organization is closely aligned with the BGF; in fact it claims to be the BGF," Conine said.

Bryant and his brother, Stanley, who police say is second in command of the Valley drug gang, were charged in 1982 in the contract killing of a man who vandalized one of their cars after buying $150 worth of cocaine that he thought was of poor quality, according to court records.

Charged as the triggerman in that shooting was Armstrong, an ex-convict who had moved to Pacoima from St. Louis and had "gained a reputation for being a hit man," court records state.

But after a preliminary hearing, the charges against the Bryant brothers were dismissed when a judge ruled there was insufficient evidence that they had ordered the killing. Armstrong later pleaded guilty to voluntary manslaughter and was sent to prison for six years.

Narcotics detectives began to focus intensively on the Bryant Organization after the murder case was dismissed, records show. Police said they identified three houses owned by Jeffrey Bryant, including the house in the 11400 block of Wheeler Avenue, where cocaine was being sold. Police said the drug operation was directed from a pool hall on Van Nuys Boulevard in Pacoima.

The drug houses were virtual fortresses; bars covered windows, and steel doors opened into cages, which cocaine buyers entered to do business, police said. Money was exchanged for cocaine through slots in the cages.

Stanley Bryant recruited people to work in the houses for $25 an hour, court records show. The workers were locked inside for eight-hour shifts. In each house, a pot filled with oil simmered 24 hours a day. Workers were instructed to dump cocaine in the oil should a police raid occur.

In the first two months of 1985, police raided the three cocaine fortresses, made several arrests and confiscated weapons and small amounts of cocaine. Evidence obtained from the raids was used to charge Jeffrey Bryant with operating drug houses. In 1986 he pleaded guilty to one of the charges and was sentenced to four years in prison.

But with the group's leader imprisoned in San Diego, the organization did not wane, police said. Stanley Bryant headed the ring on the outside while his brother pulled strings from his prison cell, police said. Investigators said they think Jeffrey Bryant has commanded the organization by telephone and through organization members who visit him in prison.

Police have identified nearly 200 people associated with the group. Intelligence files contain a pyramid-type diagram of the organization's structure. Jeffrey Bryant's name is at the top, followed by four levels of increasingly larger groupings. Those listed on the diagram range from organization lieutenants to drug distributors, rock house operators and finally street-sales people.

Whereas those in the top levels are thought to be associated with the BGF, those on the bottom are mostly members of teen-age street gangs, police said. The street gangs are recruited to sell drugs so that higher-echelon members of the organization are protected, police said.

"This is how the leaders insulate themselves," said a detective familiar with the case. "The people on the bottom are just fodder. If they get arrested, it's easy to get someone to take their place."

But the insulation broke down with the Aug. 28 killings at the Wheeler Avenue house, police said.

Detectives said the cause of the four killings relates to the 1982 killing that resulted in a dismissal for the Bryants and imprisonment for Armstrong.

Armstrong was released from prison in April. Police said he returned to St. Louis briefly, but early this summer moved to the Pacoima area with a friend, James Brown.

Investigators think that Armstrong was angry with the Bryant Organization because it had reneged on a promise to support his wife while he was in prison.

Police said a meeting was scheduled between Armstrong and the top members of Bryant's group at which Armstrong intended not only to demand a top spot in the organization but the money he thought his wife should have received.

But before the meeting took place, Armstrong, Brown, English and her daughter were ambushed. Their bodies were quickly removed from the property and dumped elsewhere. The house was empty by the time police arrived, after receiving calls from neighbors.

It was another four weeks before police had gathered evidence of what happened and began arresting the lieutenants in the Bryant Organization.

Times staff writer Claudia Puig contributed to this story.

MASSIVE DRUG, MURDER CASE
INCHES ITS WAY TOWARD TRIAL

Courts: Charges against the so-called Bryant Organization grew out of 1988 slayings. Getting verdicts may take years.

April 19, 1992

With its 10 defendants, 58 volumes of investigative records containing 20,000 pages, and 34 defense attorneys, prosecutors and investigators, the Bryant Organization murder and drug conspiracy case moves through the justice system like an elephant.

Its sheer bulk dictates that it move slowly.

Already nearly 4 years old, the massive prosecution resulted from the slayings of three adults and a child at a Lake View Terrace house where the proceeds from a $500,000-a-month rock cocaine business were allegedly counted. And the end is nowhere near.

Deputy Dist. Atty. Jan L. Maurizi, the lead prosecutor in the case, said the criminal trial of the 10 people charged with either the slayings or with taking part in a conspiracy to control the crack trade in the northeast San Fernando Valley could make U.S. legal history.

"I think there is every possibility that it will be the longest and most expensive trial ever," Maurizi, who has been working full-time on the case for most of the last three years, said last week.

A trial date for the case has not been set. Court officials have not found a courtroom that will be available — and big enough — for a trial expected to last by some estimates as long as three years.

Bills for the taxpayer-paid attorneys representing both sides in the case run nearly $2,000 per hour when court is in session. The prosecution's investigation has already cost at least $2 million, by one defense attorney's estimate.

And when a courtroom is chosen for the trial, there will undoubtedly be renovations. Bulletproof glass partitions will be added for security. Bleacher seats will likely be built to allow all of the attorneys and defendants a clear view of the witness stand. All of it will add to the cost of the case.

Once the logistics of where and when are set, the complexities will continue. The case may require more than one jury, and the selection process may take months. Each witness who takes the stand will be subject to cross-examination by 10 attorneys representing the different defendants. Since four defendants face a possible death penalty, a lengthy penalty phase could follow any convictions.

The landmark case for such lengthy and costly prosecutions was the McMartin Pre-School molestation case. The first of two Los Angeles trials in the McMartin case lasted 32 months from the start of jury selection until the return of verdicts. The bill to taxpayers was estimated at $15 million.

The murder and drug case is the result of a sweeping investigation of the so-called Bryant Organization, named for two Pacoima brothers who allegedly headed the group. The investigation began after the Aug. 28, 1988, shootings on Wheeler Avenue.

Also known on the streets as The Family, the organization had as many as 200 associates and had controlled much of the flow of cocaine to the northeast San Fernando Valley since 1982, according to the charges against the defendants.

Maurizi said the group also was extraordinarily violent in maintaining a grip on its territory. She blames the organization for 25 murders over the past 10 years.

Those killed in the 1988 shootings were Andre Louis Armstrong, 31; James Brown, 43; Lorretha English, 23, and her 2-year-old daughter, Chemise. Investigators said the killings occurred at a time when the Bryant group was fending off competition and demands for money from Armstrong, a former associate who had recently been released from prison.

According to authorities, Armstrong was set up to be killed when he was lured to a meeting at the organization's "cash" house on Wheeler Avenue. Armstrong and Brown were shot to death as they entered the house. A gunman then ran out to their car and shot English and her daughter. The little girl was executed with a point-blank shot to the back of the head.

Within six weeks of the slayings, squads of officers

with search warrants raided 26 houses where suspected members of the Bryant Organization lived or did business. Investigators said they recovered numerous records detailing the group's drug business — which grossed at least $1.6 million quarterly.

Evidence from the raids and the shooting scene and information from a key member of the organization who agreed to cooperate with authorities led to charges being filed against 12 people believed to make up the top leadership and enforcement arms of the organization.

Among those charged is Stanley Bryant, now 34, the alleged leader of the group at the time because his older brother, Jeff, was in prison. Also among the defendants is Le Roy Wheeler, 23, a suspected hit man for The Family who authorities said ran to the car where English and her daughter were sitting and dispatched them with a shotgun and handgun.

Because it took three years to round up all 12 suspects, six separate preliminary hearings — some lasting months — and a grand jury session have been held during the past few years. It wasn't until September that the last suspect was ordered to stand trial.

Earlier this month, two of the defendants pleaded guilty to drug and aiding and abetting charges, the first convictions in the case. One was put on probation after spending the last 18 months in jail. The other has not yet been sentenced.

What remains to be decided on is a date for the trial — and a venue.

"We still haven't found a home," said Maurizi, explaining that a Los Angeles Superior Court judge who has been hearing pretrial motions in the case has been reassigned to civil matters, leaving the Bryant case without a courtroom.

With trial length estimates running from Maurizi's conservative one year to as long as three years, courtrooms with clear dockets are difficult to find. Finding a courtroom large enough is also a problem. During pretrial hearings the defendants and attorneys have filled audience seats and jury boxes.

But that extra room won't be there during the trial. Steve Flanagan, an attorney representing defendant Tannis Curry, said the case may require two or more juries because evidence against some defendants cannot be heard by jurors considering different charges against other defendants.

"I think at a minimum we are looking at two juries and possibly even more," he said.

Maurizi said a courtroom may have to be renovated for the case. She also said all of the logistic problems may make it so unwieldy that the defendants will have to be tried separately — possibly in simultaneous trials.

However, the prosecutor said she opposes breaking up the defendants and hopes the case will find a home soon in one of six courtrooms used for "long cause" cases in downtown Los Angeles or the four courtrooms used for that purpose in Van Nuys. She believes that the trial may finally start by early fall — four years after the killings.

Attorneys involved said the trial is expected to be lengthy because of the complex conspiracy charges, which require a massive amount of documentary evidence as well as testimony. Also, having so many defendants automatically lengthens the process.

"With 10 defendants there could be 10 attorneys conducting cross-examinations of every witness," Maurizi said.

"The more defendants you have, the length of trial increases geometrically, not arithmetically," said Ralph Novotney, who represents defendant Donald Smith. "I think somebody even said this would last four years. I think one to two years is realistic."

Flanagan said jury selection alone could take months. Between the prosecution and all of the defendants, there will be more than 200 challenges to jurors allowed, he added.

"I have no idea how long it will take," Flanagan said of the trial. "As a general rule, a prosecutor's estimate is conservative. If she says one year, I would at least double it."

In addition to the defendants, the case has a massive attachment of attorneys and investigators. There are 17 defense attorneys — all court-appointed. Seven defendants have been granted two attorneys each because they face the death penalty or life in prison if convicted. Each defendant also has at least one court-appointed investigator.

On the prosecution side, Maurizi heads a team of four deputy district attorneys and four investigators, including Los Angeles Police Detective James Vojtecky, the lead investigator since the beginning of the case.

Most of the prosecutors and investigators have been working full-time on the case for a year or longer. They primarily work out of an office near the San Fernando Courthouse, its location kept secret for security reasons. In the course of the investigation, members of the team have traveled to 11 states to interview witnesses and gather evidence.

While most murder cases result in investigators accumulating reports and other documents that fill two or three thick blue binders called "murder books," the Bryant case has filled 58 so far. During one preliminary hearing, they were lined up in the unused jury box so they could be easily referred to by prosecutors. Side by side, they stretched more than 10 feet.

"It's a nightmare when you try to get everything collated," Flanagan said. "I have attempted to computerize everything. But there is so much. There are approximately 20,000 pages. There are thousands and thousands of telephone numbers."

It is difficult to estimate how much has been spent on the case or how much taxpayers will eventually have to pay. The investigation of the shooting involved numerous law enforcement agencies, and at times as many as 200 officers were brought in to conduct searches. Flanagan estimated the investigation has cost more than $2 million. Maurizi said that estimate could be in the ballpark, but she could not confirm it.

The true costs of the case would include the salaries of prosecutors, police investigators, bailiffs, judges and court staff. The defendants' attorneys are each paid about $100 an hour. At that rate, a year in trial — minus a two-week vacation — will cost taxpayers more than $3.5 million for defense attorneys alone.

Defense attorneys said the cost of the trial should not be criticized because the defendants are constitutionally guaranteed competent counsel and a fair trial. They said the prosecution has set the stage for the lengthy and expensive battle by alleging complicated conspiracy charges.

"Millions have been spent on their investigation," Flanagan said. "I don't think anybody can quibble over the money" spent on defense attorneys.

Novotney said that if the prosecution dropped some of the "garbage charges" against the defendants, such as the allegation that the organization was involved in a drug conspiracy, the trial and costs would be greatly trimmed.

"The cost of justice sometimes is expensive," Novotney said. "This is a megacase. I have a client who faces a possible death penalty. I have an obligation to prepare the best defense possible. It's an expensive proposition."

Citing confidentiality, he declined to say what his defense team has been paid in the 1½ years he has been on the case.

Maurizi said the length of the case works to the advantage of the defendants as well as their attorneys. As a case drags on, the prosecution's evidence can unravel.

"Memories fade to a certain extent, evidence can be lost or destroyed," she said. "In this case, there has always been a great danger factor to our witnesses."

Vojtecky said one of the case's defendants, Nash Newbil, 56, had been free on bail awaiting trial but was then jailed in September when he allegedly directed an assault against a witness in the case. Newbil was charged with assault for allegedly ordering two men to hold down the witness and inject a hallucinogenic drug into her tongue with a hypodermic needle. During the alleged attack, Newbil called her a "snitch," police said.

Defense attorney Flanagan countered that the slow movement of the case causes defendants an enormous hardship.

"It's a nightmare for those individuals," he said. "There is a presumption of innocence, but they languish in jail.

"I don't think it is anybody's fault. There is an investigation that has been done by both sides. I don't think anybody is trying to hold it up."

NOTE: The sheer size of the prosecution spawned by the quadruple murder in Lake View Terrace proved to be unmanageable. The case was eventually pared down and split. Still, over the next five years there were several prosecutions and convictions of members of the Bryant Family Organization for crimes ranging from murder to drug dealing and money laundering. Stanley Bryant and two others were eventually sent to death row for the killings. His brother, Jeffrey Bryant, was returned to prison as well after being convicted of drug-related crimes. By 1997, the organization most responsible for bringing rock cocaine to the northeast Valley was completely dismantled and irrelevant, according to police and federal authorities.

HIGH TIME

BILLY THE BURGLAR

SOUTH FLORIDA SUN-SENTINEL
June 7, 1987

BILLY SCHROEDER is 24 years old. But he looks, at his best, like 24 going on 40. Put him up next to his boyish mug shot of just a few years ago and the boy is long gone. The bleached blond hair has turned to brown and shows signs of thinning. The body, too, is thin, having been tapered by its addictions. Sometimes the eyes, set in a ruddy face, are glassy and have a thousand-yard stare in a six-by-six room.

Permanent blue ink wraps around both his arms. The lion, the hawk, the skull. He wears his philosophy — his former philosophy, mind you — forever beneath his sleeve: the man with a dope pipe, the inscription "Get High" on his biceps. All of it the work of jailhouse tattoo artists.

Looking at Billy Schroeder, it is easy to imagine what a nightmare it would have been for someone to have come home to find this stranger inside. Though on occasion that did occur, hundreds of times in the last year Schroeder was in and out of homes without being seen. He was a burglar, one of the most prolific that local police have known about in recent years.

For a time, it seemed as though nothing could stop him. He cruised through the streets of South Broward and North Dade, through the back doors and windows of up to five homes a day. Fueled by cocaine or the craving for it, he broke into at least 350 homes in a year's time and stole an estimated $2 million worth of property.

DESPITE THE big numbers he posted, Schroeder was no master burglar. He lived high and blew every dollar he got. He was just another crack addict, who in actuality was not as good as he was lucky. Locked up now, even he will tell you that. And he'll tell you that his luck worked against him as much as it worked for him.

"I guess I was a good burglar, but it seemed like I was

lucky more than anything," he says. "I was sloppy. It seems if they really wanted me, they could have gotten me sooner. I wish now that they would have. My good luck was really bad luck, I guess."

Burglary is a mid-level crime, meaning that on a seriousness scale it is far below murder, somewhere above petty theft. Also meaning it inspires similar priorities in most police departments and prosecutors' offices.

Still, burglary is a crime that cuts across social strata, leaving its scars on the poor and the rich, the young and the old. And it is one of the most prevalent of crimes in our society. In Broward County there were 25,000 burglaries last year; 22,000 in Palm Beach County. Across Florida it happened more than 250,000 times. Only 16 percent of the cases were cleared by arrest.

The story of one of the most prolific burglars in Broward is not just a story of a man's addiction to a drug and what that drug made him do. He is part of an epidemic. And the proper way to tell Billy Schroeder's tale is to also tell the stories of those he stole from, and those who hunted him.

BILLY SCHROEDER was born and raised in the blue-collar Lake Forest area west of Hollywood. He grew up in a home with a mother and sister, and sometimes he lived with his grandparents. There was no father in the house after he turned four. He learned about authority and manhood on the streets. And by the time he was 11 the streets had already led him into the sampling of drugs and burglary. It was during his 11th year that he was caught for the first time: he was inside a neighbor's home, and placed on juvenile probation.

From there he moved deeper into a life of drug use and thievery. He was kicked out of Hallandale High School for dealing the drug THC in the bathrooms. He was arrested selling Quaaludes to an undercover cop.

Incarceration may have been the best thing for Schroeder, but he avoided prison and always won the second chance. That changed in 1981 when, at 17, he was sent as an adult to DeSoto Correctional Institute for burglary. In prison, he finished high school, took carpentry classes, got his tattoos, temporarily ended his addiction to drugs and, most of all, waited for his release. That came in late 1984 and he returned to his old neighborhood.

Schroeder says he stayed clean for more than a year, working first as a gas station attendant and then using his prison-learned skills as a carpenter. When he was tempted by the old life of drugs and thievery he would carefully unfold the prison release papers he kept in his wallet.

"Every time I was slipping I would look at my papers," he says. "I didn't want to go back. I looked at them and said I'd earned my freedom and paid my debt."

But by the end of 1985, Billy Schroeder had misplaced his papers and he started slipping. And one night a friend came by his apartment and introduced him to co-caine in the form called crack. Within 24 hours of smok-ing his first rock, all that Schroeder had learned was gone. So was his TV and stereo and living room furni-ture, all traded for crack. A week later the job was gone, too. Urges controlled Billy Schroeder again. His first break-in was into the house next door.

Schroeder quickly became re-addicted to both drugs and burglary. The two were the all-consuming parts of his life. He could not have one without the other. He began cruising the neighborhoods of South Broward wearing a phony Florida Power & Light shirt and carry-ing a screwdriver.

On Easter Sunday 1986 Gladys Jones became one of Billy Schroeder's statistics. The revelation came to her like a cold finger running down her spine when she opened the front door of the home where she lived alone near Hollywood. Immediately she saw the doors of the dining room buffet standing open and its contents spilled on the floor. She turned to the left and saw the empty shelf in the living room, the TV gone.

She knew right away what had happened. It came to her with the weakness in her knees and the catch in her breath. Gladys, who is in her 60s and asked that her real name not be used, turned and ran.

It was two hours before she returned. That was after

the police searchers had come and gone, the K-9 dog had come and gone, and her son-in-law had even searched the house. Gladys walked unsteadily into her home to learn what the invader had taken. She found that the floors were covered with things apparently considered by the burglar and then discarded. The jewelry boxes were dumped on the bed, Gladys' underwear drawer had been rifled, and the Easter basket for her grand-daughter was turned over on the kitchen floor.

About halfway through this sad inventory she realized that mostly it was her peace of mind that had been taken. She asked her daughter to stay with her. She couldn't sleep alone in the house.

Broward County Sheriff's Investigator Bill Cloud has worked burglary cases for nine years. His experience has taught him two constants: That nowadays almost all burglars break into homes to get money for drugs, and that drug-fueled burglars do very careless work — to the point of hitting homes in their own neighborhoods be-fore moving on to other areas.

When in early 1986 Cloud began getting a number of similar Lake Forest burglary cases dropped on his desk, he figured he had one burglar out there hitting homes at a fast pace. So he took to the neighborhood streets and culled a list of suspects' names from the steady cast of in-formants he maintains.

One of the names was Billy Schroeder's. Cloud ran it through the crime computer and learned of Schroeder's rap sheet. He then asked the Sheriff's Office crime lab for a "zone run," a comparison between Schroeder's finger-prints and those found at burglaries in the patrol zone that included Lake Forest. It was a request that would take weeks because of the backlog of requests to the crime lab. While he was waiting, Cloud distributed fliers bearing Billy Schroeder's 1983 mug shot to deputies and South Broward police departments. And he went out looking.

BILLY SCHROEDER worked enviable hours, usually less than five hours a day. He worked when he had to, when the cocaine ran low and his body's craving for it ran high. He would put on the FPL shirt and cap that he had had made at a flea market T-shirt concession, and clip a can of Mace to his belt. The getup made him a meter reader. He would drive a borrowed car through neighborhoods before and after lunch — 9 to 11 and 2 to 4 — the best times of finding empty homes. After spotting a target house he would just knock on the front door.

If somebody answered, Schroeder was ready with a variety of lines and would then move on. But if the knock went unanswered, he'd go around back — a meter reader doing his job — and break in after checking for alarm systems. With his screwdriver he was an expert at breaking locks and windowpanes, removing jalousie windows. He knew how to pop a sliding glass door in just the way that it would crumble into a pile of glass dust without noise enough to alert a neighbor.

Once inside, first to consider was the refrigerator, full of all the food he had neglected while binging on crack. After a snack, he'd grab a bag or a pillowcase, and then there were all those drawers and cabinets and hiding places to find. It was a quick operation: 10, maybe 15 minutes max. Cash and jewelry, guns if there were any, and on the way out he'd grab the big stuff, a TV or a VCR or both, the hot trade items in the crack houses of South Florida. "I didn't care about being seen by neighbors or anybody," he says. One time he broke in the front door of a home while a woman was watering flowers across the street. He just ran when she yelled. Once while driving through Miramar he saw a lighted Christmas tree through the front window of a house. He backed his car up, broke through the front window and loaded his car with gifts from beneath the tree, going back three times for more.

AFTER EVERY DAY of burglary, Billy headed to the crack houses west of Hollywood to trade his goods. The drug peddlers who worked the perimeters of the houses called him the "gold man" because of the jewelry he always had for trade. On a good day, he'd have loot from four or five homes.

Schroeder kept nothing he stole, turned everything into crack and the cash he needed to pay for the hotel rooms where he binged on cocaine, crashed and hid. Detective Cloud estimates that if Schroeder stole $2 million in merchandise, his return was not much better than a dime on the dollar: a few hundred thousand dollars' worth of cash and drugs.

"Almost every single day I was robbing another family," Schroeder says. "It started with one burglary a day to support my habit for the day. I needed $200. Then it got to be $300 and I had to rob two houses. Then it got to be $500 a day and four houses and on and on from there.

"It got to be a game. I didn't care about anything else. I would drive down a street and decide, Eenie, meenie, minie, moe, that's the house I'm going to do.

"I was living for my drug. It was my life, my future. I spent every penny I had on it.

"And I was scared. I figured the cops were looking for me because of my prints so I was living in hotels, moving almost every day. I never came out except to rob another house or get drugs. I would stay in the room behind a chain, a deadbolt and a desk pushed up against the door."

THE ZONE RUN with Billy Schroeder's fingerprints that Detective Cloud had asked for came back with several positive IDs. Cloud asked the State Attorney's Office for a felony warrant, a request that would take several weeks to go through the legal morass. Still, Cloud was now sure who his man was. He just had to find him.

Meanwhile, detectives in other departments — Hollywood, Hallandale, Miramar and North Miami — were learning that Schroeder was an increasingly active break-in artist.

"It got so that I could just pick up a burglary report and be able to tell Billy had been there," says Hallandale Detective Dermot Mangan. "When it was a daytime job with the place ransacked and food eaten, it was usually him.

"We were all looking for him," recalls Cloud. "I once got word that he was going to a certain store to cash a check. I waited in there and when he saw a man in a jacket and tie he ran. He was so paranoid, anybody in a suit was a cop. That time he just happened to be right. We kept just missing him like that. At the motels, on the streets. Sometimes by minutes. It became a mission to get him."

GLADYS JONES spent the time after the burglary arranging for new lights to be placed outside her home, having the bushes cut away from the windows, putting steel mesh screens over every window.

"I hate it," she says. "The house looks awful and it makes me feel like I'm the prisoner when I'm the victim. I'm still afraid to be here by myself."

One night long after the burglary, Gladys was dressing for an evening out when she reached into her jewelry box for a certain gold necklace. It was gone, one of the belongings she hadn't noticed missing after the burglary. The discovery brought the whole thing, the intrusion, the loss, the anger, all back down on her. Most of all it rekindled the fear.

Gladys started counting the days left until her retirement from her office job in two years. That would be when she would put her house up for sale and move away from South Florida. But, still, at night, she would lie awake in bed and listen. . . . She would return from outings, unlock the door, stand there and listen. . . .

Often when home alone, she found herself asking, did I just hear a noise out there or is it my imagination? The legacy of fear that Billy Schroeder left behind will remain with her always, she says.

Billy Schroeder could have gotten away. On one job, in North Dade, he hit the jackpot — a pile of jewelry that he converted to bags of cash and crack.

"I ended up with $20,000 cash in my hands," he recalls. "I said to my girlfriend, 'Let's get out of here. I have the money now, let's go to a rehab center and get off this.'"

They decided on New Jersey, even got the airline tickets. But on the way to the airport, Billy and his girlfriend went to a friend's house to say good-bye. And they celebrated the good-bye with one more rock. Within a few hours Billy checked into a Hilton suite with a bag full of rocks. Within days the jackpot money was gone.

Schroeder wouldn't get another chance to get away. His habit was growing and costing him close to $1,000 a day. He was breaking into more homes each day and the risks were getting greater while he was getting sloppier. He even stopped wearing his phony FPL uniform.

On Feb. 26, 1987, Davie Police got a call about a possible burglary in process. Officers went to the home and saw an open window, and a screen leaning against the outside wall. The screen was the giveaway. A few minutes later the cops entered the house and found a burglar hiding in a bathroom shower stall. He said his name was William Burns.

As the Davie officers were booking the burglar into the county jail, a sheriff's deputy booking his own prisoner looked over at Burns and recognized him as the man on the wanted fliers Detective Cloud had been circulating for almost a year.

"You're not William Burns," the deputy said, and the long crime spree of Billy Schroeder was over.

THE COPS who wanted to speak to Schroeder had to take turns. It took two days for the elusive burglar to come out of his cocaine intoxication and figure out he was in jail, but when he did, he considered his lot — the fingerprints, the evidence, his past record — and simply said, "Let's go. I want it behind me."

Schroeder sat handcuffed and shackled in the back-seats of several detectives' cars as they drove through neighborhoods of South Florida. It took him three weeks to go over the territory, pointing out the houses he remembered being in. The detectives matched Schroeder's recollections against their own burglary reports. All told, Cloud says they cleared close to 350 burglaries. And there are perhaps dozens of others Schroeder can't remember.

Of the millions of dollars in property that Schroeder stole, nothing was recovered. "It's gone forever," Cloud says.

Schroeder was charged with 13 burglaries. (It would take years to prosecute him if he were charged in all his burglaries.) On May 21, he tearfully pleaded guilty to the charges in a plea agreement that could leave him facing as many as 20 years in prison.

"I want to get this behind me," he told the judge. "I have to look to the future."

While waiting for that future, he has been kept in the east wing of the North Broward Detention Complex, home to all inmates undergoing drug counseling and detoxification. Schroeder takes part in the jail's "New Life" programs, works in the laundry and volunteers to speak to visiting groups of teenagers about the dangers of drugs.

He seems resigned to a lengthy stint in prison. And he seems genuinely repentant. Still, he can only gain by this contrition and therefore his sincerity is open to question.

But he cries when he talks about the time more than a year ago that he smoked that first rock. And he cries when he talks about the families he stole from. He says maybe someday he will make restitution, a possibility that is, in reality, laughable.

"I just want to do something," he says. "I think about all the families I robbed and I know I've got to do something for them."

Like many a jail inmate, Schroeder says he has got Jesus with him now. He tries to keep his sleeve over the "Get High" tattoo and regrets the day he got it. He says he wants another chance. That's the bottom line: another chance. But deep down, he knows it might be too late for Billy Schroeder.

"I'm hoping to someday get another shot at society," he says. "I don't want to be thrown completely away."

Billy Schroeder turned his back on society but now hopes it won't do the same to him. He seeks sympathy for the devil, so to speak. But it is hard to come by.

"I like Billy Schroeder," says Detective Bill Cloud. "But I have no sympathy for him. I have sympathy for the people he stole from. They have to put up with the feelings of intrusion and their losses for the rest of their lives. They worked all their lives so they can have some of these possessions, and somebody breaks in and it's all gone."

Those sentiments are echoed like the clanging of a jail door: "He was destroying people with what he did," Detective Dermot Mangan says. "He has got to pay something for that."

"It's sad," says burglary victim Gladys Jones. "Sure the kid needs help. But the people he hurt also need something. When I think of what I've been through and that I'm only one of the hundreds of people he did this to, I still feel very angry and hurt."

Lawyer Norman Elliott Kent, who was appointed to defend Schroeder after he confessed to his crimes, declines to use pat arguments like drugs made Schroeder do it, he's a product of his environment, he deserves a break and so on. Much of that is valid, but somewhere along the line Billy Schroeder made a choice. There is responsibility somewhere.

"Billy was a drug addict and drug money burns quickly," Kent says. "And for all that he managed to steal, there is nothing left but hurt victims and a troubled defendant. All Billy has to show for it is his empty pockets, his drug addiction and a jail term. If there is a lesson in all of this, that is it: to let people know what can happen. His message is that in the end everybody loses."

IT'S MORNING in the east wing and a small group of high school students are gathered in the multi-purpose room for a tour of the jail. With all the banging of the heavy doors, sharp clacking of electronic locks and echoes bouncing off the steel and concrete, the students have to lean forward to hear the speaker.

The speaker is an inmate here, a young man with a prematurely aged face. He is here to tell them that he is a loser who found out how to win, how to make it the right way too late. Don't be like me, he wants to tell them.

"Hello, my name is Bill," he begins. "And I'm a drug abuser.

"I started doing drugs when I was 11 years old. And pretty soon after that I started going through people's windows. I hurt a lot of people. And here I am. . . ."

LYING IN WAIT

AMBUSH SHOOTING

Nurse killed trying to aid man on street.

LOS ANGELES TIMES
February 23, 1989

A PRIVATE NURSE who stopped her car in the hills above Studio City and apparently got out to help a man lying in the street was fatally shot Wednesday when the man stood up and pulled a gun, Los Angeles police said.

No arrest was made in the ambush killing of 40-year-old Lucille Marie Warren at Montcalm Avenue and Woodrow Wilson Drive in an exclusive neighborhood of hillside homes.

Warren was shot at 6:45 a.m. while on her way home to Inglewood, police said. She had left a house on Montcalm where she worked as a night nurse.

Investigators said there were indications that she was the specific target of the fatal attack and may even have known her killer. Detectives are investigating whether Warren, who was divorced and lived with her two teen-age children, was involved in any personal disputes that could have led to the shooting.

"This doesn't appear to be a random encounter," said homicide Detective Mike Coffey.

Motive Unknown

While the motive for the shooting was unknown, police said, the killer may have been in the street because he knew that Warren was approaching and would stop if she thought someone needed help.

"She was a nurse," said Lt. Ron LaRue. "If you knew she was a nurse, you could find a way to make her stop. The suspect was lying in the street and she stopped."

Warren had been working at the home in the Mont-calm cul-de-sac at least two months, police said. Officials of a Van Nuys–based registry of nurses, through which police said Warren was referred to jobs, declined to comment.

Detectives would not name the person for whom Warren worked. Los Angeles real estate records list the large, gated property where police said she cared for a patient as belonging to Miklos Rozsa, 81, a composer and three-time Academy Award winner for the musical scoring of films.

After finishing her night's work, Warren was leaving the cul-de-sac when she stopped at Woodrow Wilson Drive after seeing the man in the middle of the street, police said.

Gun Pulled from Clothing

When Warren got out and walked toward the front of the car, the man stood up and pulled a handgun out of his clothing. Police said they do not know whether the pair spoke before the man fired several times at Warren.

Warren was hit by gunfire at least twice, including once in the head, and fell mortally wounded in the street, police said. One other shot hit the windshield of her car, which eventually rolled into an embankment on the other side of the street. Police said the gunman ran to a car parked nearby and sped away. The victim was not robbed.

A resident called police on a car phone after seeing the woman in the street. Coffey said several residents saw parts of the crime and provided police with descriptions of the gunman, his car and the sequence of events.

Warren was taken to St. Joseph Medical Center in Burbank, where she died at 10:48 a.m., police said.

As police cordoned off the area, residents gathered nearby or watched from their windows. Police said the shooting, which occurred near a corner house owned by artist David Hockney, was unusual in the quiet, affluent neighborhood.

"Violence is getting common all over the city," said a man who declined to give his name. "People pay a lot of money to get away from it but it doesn't always work."

Times staff writer Amy Pyle contributed to this story.

NOTE: Lucille Warren's former boyfriend was arrested, tried and convicted of murdering her. A former probation officer, he was sentenced to 27 years in prison. Of note in the sentencing was that the killer avoided the death penalty because the judge in the case ruled that he had not been lying in wait, a special circumstance that would have made him eligible for the death penalty. The judge ruled that the lying in wait statute was drawn in regard to killers who hide and then surprise their victims. Since the killer was lying on the street in plain sight when Warren approached he was not hiding and was therefore not lying in wait.

TRUNK MUSIC

WHO SHOT VIC WEISS?

A trail gone cold.

LOS ANGELES TIMES
June 11, 1989

THE MEETING WITH Jack Kent Cooke and Jerry Buss had gone well. Vic Weiss was close to a deal that would bring University of Nevada, Las Vegas, basketball coach Jerry Tarkanian to Los Angeles to lead the Lakers, the team Cooke was selling to Buss.

Briefcase in hand, the stocky but energetic Weiss, a 51-year-old sports promoter, sometime agent and businessman, left the meeting room at a Beverly Hills hotel, hopped into his Rolls-Royce and headed over the hill to his house in Encino.

But Weiss never made it home. Three days later, on June 17, 1979, his red-and-white Rolls-Royce was spotted in the garage of a North Hollywood hotel.

People opened the trunk and there was the body of Victor J. Weiss, hands tied behind his back. He had been killed with two gunshots to the head.

Organized Crime Link

Ten years later, Weiss' killing remains unsolved and one of the San Fernando Valley's most puzzling mysteries. Los Angeles police believe Weiss was the victim of an organized crime hit, the most difficult of murder cases to crack.

It is a case that plunged detectives into the milieu of mobsters and informants, where they became suspicious of everyone, sometimes even fellow cops. And once they even found themselves being followed by someone they were investigating.

Still, they were able to learn much about the secret life of Vic Weiss. They learned that while he publicly hobnobbed with legitimate names in sports and business, he privately rubbed shoulders with criminals, ran up huge debts on sports betting and skimmed off the top of laundered money he delivered to mobsters in Las Vegas.

It is believed by police that those latter indiscretions cost Weiss his life. But who ordered the killing and who carried it out remain unknown.

Detective Leroy Orozco, the only original investigator still assigned to the killing, says that after 21 years as a homicide detective, the Weiss case tantalizes him most. He has followed leads across the country but never made an arrest. He has carefully investigated and traced potential suspects, only to learn that, apparently by grim coincidence, they too had been killed.

Orozco has two file drawers filled with reports, notes and evidence on the case to show for a decade of investigation. But even after 10 years, he doesn't need to open the boxes to recall the details. He can even recall what he was doing — driving his family to an ice cream parlor after a Father's Day dinner — when his electronic pager beeped and he was called to the parking garage in North Hollywood.

"This case has been my biggest challenge," Orozco said. "It won't lie down and die.

"You get a case like this maybe once in a lifetime. How often do you read about a Mafia hit, especially in L.A., with the intrigue of Vegas and the cops being followed by the bad guys? But I knew from the beginning it would be tough. As soon as I walked into that garage and saw that Rolls, I knew I was in deep."

In life, Vic Weiss presented the image of success. Raised in the Pasadena area — where he went to high school with longtime friend Tarkanian — Weiss first became successful in real estate and insurance ventures and was later known as a part owner in Ford and Rolls-Royce dealerships in Van Nuys. His red-and-white Rolls had a gold interior. He wore a diamond ring and a Rolex watch. He was known as a guy who always picked up the tab after dinner or drinks with friends and business associates.

Sports Negotiations a Hobby

Weiss became prominent in sports circles beginning in 1973 when he bought the contract of welterweight boxing contender Armando Muniz. Though not a professional sports agent, Weiss handled contract negotiations for his friend Tarkanian as a hobby. It was that hobby that brought him to the negotiating table with Cooke and Buss at the Beverly Comstock Hotel on June 14, 1979.

According to police accounts of the meeting, details of the agreement to bring Tarkanian to the Lakers were written by Weiss and Cooke on a piece of paper that Weiss dropped into his briefcase when he left.

"He was probably confident as he left," Orozco says. "Negotiations went well."

Weiss was to go to dinner with his wife, Rose, but first, police say, he planned to call Tarkanian, who was waiting at a Long Beach hotel for word on the negotiations.

Tarkanian never got the call, and the talks would never go further. The Lakers eventually hired another coach.

Weiss was reported missing by his wife, but there was no sign of him until four days later when a security guard spotted his Rolls in the garage of the Sheraton Universal hotel. After Weiss' decomposed body was discovered and removed, detectives found no clues to what had happened.

Weiss' wallet and briefcase were gone, but his diamond ring and watch had not been taken. That led police to rule out robbery as a motive. Cooke, Buss and Tarkanian were quickly eliminated as having any involvement. That left police with the mystery.

But the Rolls-Royce, though clean of evidence, generated a lead in the case. Several people who had learned of the slaying in the media called police and said they remembered seeing the distinctive car on the day Weiss disappeared, Orozco says. Through these witnesses, police were able to chart Weiss' path from Beverly Hills along Beverly Glen Boulevard to Ventura Boulevard and west into Encino.

Mysterious Tall Man

A witness told police that he had seen the Rolls pull to the curb on a street in Encino and a white Cadillac with three men in it stop behind. The witness said Weiss got out of his car and two men — one described as a 6-foot, 6-inch blond — got out of the Cadillac.

The witness said the blond man angrily pointed a finger in Weiss' face as he spoke to him. After a few moments Weiss got back in his car, the blond man got in the backseat behind him and the third man got in the front. Then the Rolls and the Cadillac drove away.

As detectives delved into Weiss' background, they became confident that the witness had seen Weiss' killers. They learned that Weiss maintained a lifestyle that belied his true financial worth. They learned that many of his associates were involved in organized crime.

Orozco says that Weiss had no financial interest in the car dealerships he reportedly owned; he was merely a paid consultant or promotions man. An associate owned the house where he lived in Encino, and his Rolls-Royce was leased.

"When he died, he had some insurance; that was about it," Orozco says.

Police also began receiving reports from anonymous callers, organized crime informants and Las Vegas law enforcement officers that Weiss was involved with mobsters in Nevada and Florida. The informants said Weiss had run up gambling debts.

Mob-Style Hit

The information convinced police that Weiss had been kidnapped by the three men in the Cadillac and executed in a mob-style hit.

Orozco says he and his partner, John Helvin, traced one of Weiss' close friends to central Florida, where he had moved immediately after the killing and worked as a car salesman. In exchange for his anonymity, the salesman told the detectives that he knew that Weiss had run up more than $60,000 in gambling debts in Las Vegas. To make good on the debts, he had begun flying to Las Vegas and delivering packages of cash laundered in Los Angeles, Orozco says.

Each week, the money came in a brown paper package and was placed in the trunk of Weiss' Rolls-Royce, the salesman said. Weiss would then fly to Las Vegas and back on the same day. But, the salesman said, Weiss was skimming — stealing money from the deliveries — and had been caught and warned to stop.

Orozco says detectives theorized that Weiss had not heeded the warning and was killed. They began tracking the phone records of Weiss and some of his associates. They documented connections to organized crime figures and went to Las Vegas and New Port Richey, Fla., to serve search warrants on the homes of people believed associated with the killing.

Search Fails

In Las Vegas, the detectives got a search warrant from local authorities, but the house they planned to search was empty on the morning they arrived. Orozco speculated that the suspect had been tipped off and moved out.

In New Port Richey, things also went poorly.

Orozco and Helvin arrived late one afternoon and drove by the house, which they planned to search the next day after obtaining a warrant from local authorities. The house belonged to a man suspected of being an "enforcer" with an organized crime family, Orozco says. The detectives noticed a boat in the canal out back and a black Camaro parked in front, indicating that the occupants had not been tipped to the search and were still living there.

The next morning, Orozco says, he glanced out the window of his motel room and saw the same black Camaro in a parking lot across a canal next to the motel. A man was sitting behind the wheel of the car, watching the motel.

"We flipped a coin to see who'd go out the door first," Orozco says.

Helvin lost. They drew their weapons and with Orozco covering, Helvin quickly went down to the lobby. Orozco followed, but by the time they got into a rental car, the black Camaro was gone.

Orozco says he and his partner were turned down for the search warrant because they did not have enough evidence that the suspected enforcer had been involved in the Weiss killing.

Orozco says he was paranoid when he returned to Los Angeles.

Not knowing how information about their movements had gotten to the targets of the investigation, he and Helvin stopped talking about the case to some officers inside and outside the department. Orozco says that when a retired Los Angeles detective inquired about the case, he gave the man false information. A few days later, Orozco says, an organized crime informant called with the same wrong information.

"We didn't talk to anyone after that," Orozco says. "We just came in, did our work and went home. If I went out of town on the case, I only told my lieutenant."

Orozco and Helvin continued to work full-time on the Weiss killing for two years. At least three men they investigated would become the victims of apparently unrelated slayings.

Jewel Thief

One of them was Jeffrey Rockman, whose name was found on a piece of paper in Weiss' office. Police learned that Rockman, 33, was a jewel thief who worked for a Canadian organized crime syndicate and was believed to have sold stolen property to Weiss.

But police did not find Rockman in time to question him about the killing. On April 29, 1980, he was shot to death in his Marina del Rey town house. Orozco says detectives learned that Rockman's real name was Anthony Starr and that he had been given the new identity after entering the federal witness protection program when he testified in a Detroit bank robbery case. Police believe his killing was unrelated to the Weiss case.

Ronald Launius was another thief, and a drug dealer, who police learned had associated with Weiss. Though he was investigated, there was never any evidence to connect him to the slaying.

On July 1, 1981, Launius, 37, was one of four people beaten to death in a Laurel Canyon drug den. A former Hollywood nightclub owner and his bodyguard were charged last year with killing the victims in revenge for a robbery.

Orozco says Launius earlier had been associated with Horace McKenna, a former California Highway Patrol officer who operated a string of bars featuring nude dancers. McKenna was believed by police to have ties to prostitution, counterfeiting, narcotics and gambling in the Los Angeles area.

Investigators in the Weiss case attempted to learn whether McKenna was connected to the Weiss killing but never were able to establish that the two men knew each other. McKenna was killed March 9 at the gate of his Orange County estate when a gunman fired a machine gun into the back of the limousine in which he was riding. The slaying remains unsolved.

Through the years, names contained in Weiss case files have often come up in unrelated cases, Orozco says. But detectives have never put a name on the tall blond man. Although a mob informant once told police that the men who killed Weiss were themselves killed to maintain organized crime's veil of silence, Orozco believes the killers may still be alive and free.

Helvin has retired and Orozco handles other cases. But he still gets calls from informants offering street information on the Weiss killing. And sometimes he hears from law officers who have heard of the case in the course of other investigations.

"In other unsolved cases you usually hit the wall, where you've exhausted your investigation and you put it away," he says. "This one isn't like that. You can put it away but it keeps coming back."

Orozco occasionally drives the same route Vic Weiss took on his last ride. He is waiting for the piece of data that will lead to an arrest, or the name of the blond man.

"Somebody will have to get jammed up, arrested on something else, and want to give us some help," he says wistfully.

NOTE: The Vic Weiss murder case remains unsolved.

OPEN-UNSOLVED

VALLEY POLICE PUZZLE OVER MAN'S DEATH DURING RIOTS

Crimes: The Utah worker's slaying, plus two other area killings, including of a 15-year-old boy, remain unsolved.

LOS ANGELES TIMES
May 25, 1992

SOMETHING MADE John Willers go back out there. But the reason is a mystery folded silently within a mystery.

On the night Los Angeles was torn open by the verdicts in the Rodney G. King beating case, Willers, 36, twice stepped out of the safety of his Mission Hills motel room and into the dark. The first time was with other guests curious about a car collision that was followed by shots being fired. The second time he was alone.

His body was found later in the middle of Sepulveda Boulevard. He had been shot to death in one of the most curious slayings to take place during the riots.

Now the detectives assigned to the April 29 killing, Willers' family and the Salt Lake City construction crew he had come to Los Angeles with are left to wonder who killed the quiet but friendly tile setter and why. Most of all, however, they puzzle over what drew him out into the dangerous night while most everyone else stayed safely inside.

Los Angeles police have stopped short of classifying the killing as riot-related. There is too much that remains unknown, detectives said. But for those who knew Willers, the distinction of whether or not he was a riot victim seems trivial.

"It doesn't matter," said the foreman of the construction team that Willers worked on. "Somebody shot him for no reason at all. Los Angeles is a pretty place but you can keep it. I'll be damn happy when this job is over and I'll be out of here. And I will not be back. There is just no way to cope with this. It's like being the victim of a terrorist act."

The night of April 29, Willers, who was divorced and lived by himself in Salt Lake City, was staying at the Mission Hills Inn on Sepulveda near Chatsworth Street. He had moved through several states in the West in recent years, "going wherever the work was," his foreman said.

He and the other seven members of the Kerbs Construction Co. crew had come to Los Angeles three days before the riots to do the tiling work at a supermarket under construction in Mission Hills.

Willers' foreman and another tile setter he worked with agreed to discuss the incident if their identities were not revealed. They believe that they could be targeted as witnesses even though neither actually saw the shooting or the gunman.

They said members of the Kerbs crew were in their motel rooms watching reports of rioting on television when they heard cars racing outside on Sepulveda. They then heard the crash of cars colliding, followed by shots.

Police detective Woodrow Parks said the crash occurred about 10:45 p.m. when three people in one car chased two robbery suspects in another car. The fleeing vehicle circled the motel parking lot, and then collided head-on with the other car on Sepulveda. The suspected robbers fired shots at the three people trapped in the car that was chasing them, but missed. The gunmen then fled on foot.

The incident brought many guests of the motel outside,

some just to look, some to help the injured or to direct traffic around the scene. Willers was in the crowd, according to fellow workers. He stayed outside until the injured motorists were taken by ambulances to a hospital and the police — operating under alert status because of the riots — quickly moved on. The two wrecked cars were pushed into the median of the road and left.

Willers and the other guests returned to their rooms, police said. But about half an hour later, Willers decided to go back out. He dropped by the room of two of his co-workers on the way out.

"We had the TV on and knew what was happening with the riots," said one of the men Willers visited. "We told him he better stay inside. He didn't say anything. He just left. He wanted to go out."

A few minutes later, co-workers in several rooms heard shots outside.

"It was him — they had killed him," Willers' foreman said. "People went out on the balcony and saw him lying out there in the street. He had made a bad judgment, going back out there. I don't know what he was thinking. People were shooting out there and yet he wanted to go back out."

Meanwhile, less than five miles away, police in riot gear were dispersing a crowd that had gathered in front of the Foothill Division station in Pacoima. Rocks and bottles had been thrown at police. Shots were fired into the air and nearby trash bins set on fire.

Foothill Detectives Parks and Robert Bogison left that chaotic situation and rolled to the scene of the Willers shooting. They quickly conducted the on-site investigation while a squad of eight uniformed officers ringed them and kept guard.

"We were out there trying to do the investigation, wearing bullet-proof vests, not knowing if somebody else was going to start shooting," Parks said. "We were very distracted. We had to keep one lane of traffic open and, every time a car came by, it would get a little tense."

The detectives managed to locate two people who saw two teen-agers run from the area of the shooting, Parks said. One witness had asked the teen-agers what happened and they cursed at him and kept running. The witnesses said they did not see the teen-agers carrying guns.

He said that while the teen-agers are considered suspects, there is not enough known about the shooting to classify it as riot-related. Willers was white and the two teen-agers black, but there were no other disturbances reported in the immediate area that night.

Parks is seeking additional witnesses or anyone with information about the shooting and has put together a composite drawing of one of the teen-agers.

"The killing had nothing to do with looting, rioting, the things other deaths in the city were related to," Parks said. "There is really no indication what it was about."

Other motives common in street killings were easily dismissed. Willers had not been robbed. And Parks believes that the time lapse between the slaying and the car collision and shooting indicates that the incidents were unrelated.

What the detectives are left with is a case in which the victim apparently didn't know his killer and had not even seen the shooter until moments before the slaying. The detectives said such cases are the most difficult to solve.

"We have very little to go on," Parks said last week. "In a classic murder case, you spend a lot of time with the victim's background and many times you get a direction from that. But in this case, the victim doesn't know anybody in this city. He is just a random victim of L.A. violence. It doesn't matter who he was or what he did, it's not going to lead us to his killer."

Parks said the best hope for making an arrest may be a drawing of one of the teen-agers seen by the witnesses. "It's all we've got," he said.

Police have more to go on in investigating the two other deaths in the San Fernando Valley that at least were initially counted among the 60 killings attributed to the riots.

Edward Traven, 15, was fatally shot in San Fernando about two hours before Willers. He was killed by a gunman who fired into the Cadillac he was sitting in with his brother and a friend at San Fernando Road and San Fernando Mission Boulevard.

The gunman had shouted "Where are you from?" —

a gang challenge — and police said Edward had associated with gang members. Police say his slaying was an example of a gang shooting unrelated to the riots, though members of his family have insisted that the boy's death would not have occurred if not for the atmosphere of violence spurred by the riots.

San Fernando detectives said they are attempting to identify a suspect from among the area's numerous gang members.

The killing of Imad Sharaf, 31, is also unsolved. His body was found the morning of May 3 when firefighters answered a report of a brush fire near the on-ramp to the San Diego Freeway at San Fernando Mission Boulevard. Police said Sharaf, who was a photo lab technician, had been doused with a flammable substance and set afire.

Although he, too, was listed as a riot victim, Los Angeles police believe otherwise. Investigators in that case are concentrating on Sharaf's business and personal dealings while looking for a motive and suspect.

"It was some sort of dispute, we believe," Detective Olivia Pixler said. "It seems that whoever killed him knew him."

She said the fire may have been an attempt to disguise the killing as riot-related.

The Willers killing remains the Valley case from the riot period in which police have the most tenuous grasp on what happened. And part of the mystery that sticks in the minds of those who knew Willers or are investigating his death is the reason he decided to go back outside his motel room.

"We have no idea why he went back out," Parks said. "He didn't say why to anybody. The only thing we can think of is maybe he went back out to look at the wreckage" of the cars involved in the earlier chase.

Willers' sister, Dianne Housden, suggests that her brother did not realize the danger he was in. Raised in a suburb of Portland, Ore., he lived most of his life in the Pacific Northwest and Utah, Nevada and Arizona.

"What was happening in Los Angeles was totally foreign to him," said Housden, who lives in Everett, Wash. "I think he couldn't believe what was happening and wanted maybe to go out. I think he must have thought, 'Gee, this is weird' and wanted to see. He was a free spirit. I don't think he could have known the danger he was putting himself in."

Willers' foreman agreed.

"John was a friendly, open person," the foreman said. "He comes from a place where you don't have this kind of stuff, the riot or the drive-by shooting business. He would never have thought he might be in danger. But he was."

Housden said she knew that her brother was in Los Angeles because a day before the riots began, he had called and said he was trying to locate his two teen-age children whom he had lost touch with but believed were living with his former wife in Southern California.

"He was going to try to find his kids but never got the chance," Housden said.

In Willers' suitcase, police found cards and money orders made out to the boy and girl. Housden said this week that she finally located the children, who live in Hemet, and will forward their father's last gifts.

Like Willers' fellow employees, Housden said her family has had a difficult time dealing with the death.

"We are not from an area that is violent," she said. "We were not brought up in an area like that. It's not right to have this happen to anybody, but there was no reason for this to happen to him.

"John's crime was that he was at the wrong place at the wrong time."

NOTE: The murder of John Willers remains open and unsolved.

THE NOVELIST AS REPORTER

by Michael Carlson

MICHAEL CONNELLY is a reporter. A good one. Not in the tabloid sense of someone who, like a pulp fiction writer, does whatever it takes to twist the elements of a story into a recognizable template that doesn't stretch his audience's emotions beyond the certainties in which tabloids deal. Nor is he an "investigative journalist," the modern term applied to grad school rewriters of press releases when they score a celebrity interview. He's a reporter in the best sense of the word, able to gather information and see the story buried beneath all those facts, able to sort through the impressions of all sorts of people and see how they affect those facts and, most of all, able to put it all down on paper so his reader can do the same thing.

When I began my career, I had to study the UPI style book. All the things it said about structuring a story — the famous who-what-when-where-why and how — are laid out in Connelly's stories, clearly and cleanly. He organizes his stories like a reporter should, to make sure the reader sees what he has seen. This is much more than doing a Jack Webb "just the facts, ma'am." That ability to set a story out clearly serves Connelly's greatest strengths as a reporter: his perception and his empathy.

By perception I mean the ability to see and to hear, or, better, to listen to what is being said and to see what it means. This involves the greatest skill a good reporter can have, the ability to understand people. You can't *see* a good story unless you can see where it is coming from. Too often in our world, journalists move from graduate schools into hermetically sealed newsrooms, protected by security passes and cut off from the real lives of the people about whom they are supposed to report. They've grown up in a world where the relationships are clearly delineated, the conflicts take place along a very narrow perimeter and the people they write about exist only as fodder for copy.

This is not the world cops inhabit. Not the ones who are out on the streets.

Cops know that tragedy arises from the contrast of expectations with reality. They know the real lives of the

victims they find, and the real effects of the deeds perpe-
trated by the criminals they pursue. They can't escape
that knowledge, can't put a story to bed and then go
home and sleep soundly.

The most important story in this collection, as it relates to Connelly's fiction, is "The Call," in which he
spent a week on call with the Fort Lauderdale homicide
squad. Connelly says that what he saw informed everything he has written in fiction, and if you read the story
carefully you will see how true that is. It is not just the
details of crime and investigation, but the way that
Connelly the reporter absorbs the mind-set of the cops,
internalizes it. Their fatigue becomes palpable. When
Connelly sets out the facts about how hard it will be to
solve the case, you feel the emotions of the investigators,
the frustrations that are part of their everyday life. This,
to me, is the starting point for everything we know about
Harry Bosch, and the sense of tiredness which pervades
the Bosch novels so effectively.

Empathy is not identification; there is a crucial differ-
ence. Connelly tells us that, like Bosch, he collected the
shell casings from police funerals and kept them in a jar.
He rode with cops and examined crime scenes and
corpses with them, but he is not a cop. He is a reporter,
and he manages to keep a reporter's distance from his
subjects, which allows him to see the bigger picture of
the world that they inhabit.

There is a wonderfully understated moment in a story

about the LAPD's Foreign Prosecution Unit, which pursues Mexicans who have returned to their own country as suspects in crimes committed in the United States. Connelly details the differences in Mexican law that cause civil libertarians to assert that suspects traced by the unit to Mexico may not receive the same rights they would have if they had been captured in the United States. He writes, "Ross and his fellow officers contend that a murder suspect who flees to avoid prosecution in Los Angeles is accepting the justice system of the country he runs to. 'You have to accept the risks that you have incurred by fleeing,' Moya said."

I'll bet that raised more than one wry smile, but it's the way it is reported with a straight face that makes it work: you understand exactly the cops' view of the world, especially in the face of criticism you realize they see as naïve, if well-meaning.

Connelly's empathy extends beyond the police, however, to the victims of crime, and sometimes to the criminals themselves. When you read the Wilder stories, about a South Florida serial killer who went nationwide, the story that haunts you is about the families whose daughters remain missing after a year. "We haven't gotten her past that gas station," repeats the mother of one girl, referring to the last place her daughter was seen. It's the repetition that gives the words their power to move the reader.

This combination of empathy and perception creates

an authorial position that is both detached and involved at the same time. Usually, the result of this formula is cynicism, and it has long been the bane of journalists and cops alike. Connelly's creation of Bosch, who avoids becoming a hard-boiled cynic by internalizing the pain he sees, is thus a remarkable achievement, and even more so because of the way Connelly has been able to sustain that position even when writing about Bosch in the first person, as he did to great effect when he switched to the classic first-person narration for the books in which Harry operates like a classic L.A. private detective.

ONLY ONCE, in *The Poet,* does Connelly use a journalist as his protagonist. By and large, the press does not play a major part in the Bosch series. In general reporters are treated the way Connelly himself says he was when he first arrived on the crime beat in L.A.: tolerated as an inconvenience you can't get rid of, like ants at a picnic. Harry has a police reporter he more or less trusts, but he also gets set up by the television news, and shows much less anger about it than I did on his behalf when I read *City of Bones.*

The Poet was the first of Connelly's novels that he wrote end-to-end after leaving the journalist's trade, his first non-Bosch stand-alone and, perhaps not by coincidence, his first bestseller. He has said that his major motivation was the fact that when he took away his files on unsolved murders, he realized how often killers got away with it, and he wanted to write a book in which the guy would get away and there would never be a sequel. He hadn't anticipated that audience reaction would be so strong.

If you're reading this you probably realize that eventually Connelly came around to the idea of doing a sequel. He attributed it to "recovering from my cynicism," in large part after the birth of his daughter. He has also moved from Los Angeles back to Florida, and perhaps that has something to do with the change as well.

Compare the stories written for the *South Florida Sun-Sentinel* with those done later for the *Los Angeles Times* and you can sense some serious changes within Connelly. He has said that the newsroom at the *Times* was older, the veteran journalists more cynical and with a much greater sense of their own importance. You can see why. Los Angeles is a city redolent in crime, and being the backdrop for so many movies, television shows and novels gives every crime within the city more resonance. Americans have headed west for centuries, and wound up in la-la land. Latinos head to El Norte to fulfill their dreams of making a living. Asians came to build the railroads or to flee wars. The choice of the name *Bosch* made the point metaphorically; *The Garden of Earthly Delights* ought to hang in the lobby of the *Los Angeles Times* building.

Connelly's attitude is that of an outsider rather than a native Angelino. He says he arrived for his job interview at the *Times* immediately after a major robbery, which wound up serving as the basis for *The Black Echo,* and said to himself, "Jeez, this is the place to be." Being an outsider allows him the little bit of distance he needs to observe all sides of the equation. It gives him the leeway to place the nature of the city, its history and culture, as backdrop to the equation.

In Los Angeles, his view of the police and of the world of crime itself both broaden. He gains a deeper perspective of the cop's world, both its good and bad sides. His empathy begins to be extended to the criminals, some of whom become victims themselves in that strange world of the LAPD, a sort of paramilitary bureaucracy headed by a succession of police chiefs who make Donald Rumsfeld look like Jimmy Carter.

Connelly reports both sides of the story, giving a downbeat counterpoint to the police point of view. A burglar who killed a cop in the struggle for a gun is shot and killed by the police, shot three times in the head. Twice he survives, and twice reaches miraculously for conveniently placed guns. The subtext, that he had already killed a cop, is brought to the surface, subtly but unmistakably. A car full of armed robbers shoot it out with the shotgun-wielding cops from the Special Investigations Section, who watched them rob a fast-food outlet and then surrounded them. Connelly reports the incident straightforwardly but saves for the end the revelation that the robbers were armed with unloaded pellet guns, and were thus unlikely to have chosen to shoot it out.

Harry Bosch lives within these ambiguities. His world cannot be defined, nor understood, without a feeling for the pressure under which the police operate, and the frustration endemic in the job. Understanding that helps explain the cop's instinct to close ranks and protect one's own. But cops are also part of a fiercely self-devouring bureaucracy. Think back to Connelly's original description of working at the *Los Angeles Times*. He has said that the newsroom was more like a family, with a strict sense of hierarchy, than his Florida paper, where the staff were of a similar age and socialized outside the office. This is the big leagues. So, too, with the LAPD — arguably America's most visible police department.

Some of the most satisfying scenes in the Bosch canon involve his clashes with authority, from Harvey "98" Pounds to the Bureau of Homeland Security. Bosch has no time for careerists and turf fighters; he's too busy trying to keep his integrity as he watches the dividing line between those who keep the rules and those who break them, between order and chaos, disappear. This is what Bosch goes home to. This is why he sits in dark rooms and tries to smooth it over with jazz.

• • •

THE CRIME WRITERS I most admire are the ones who do something different with the form. Hammett's accounting of people's lies, evasions and self-serving testimonies, with no stylistic value judgment coming between the character and the reader. Chandler's symphonies of simile. Marlowe's ability to crack wise in ways that don't occur to real people until the next day. Donald Westlake crafting Richard Stark's bare, clipped prose, which matches Parker's bare, clipped view of the world. George Higgins' ability to narrate through dialogue, where his characters' storytelling ability tells you more about them than any description could. James Ellroy's riffing and agonizing alliterative arsenal.

On the surface, Connelly breaks no new ground. He writes well and cleanly, but look carefully and you'll see how it goes beyond clean. His prose style is, in fact, an outgrowth of his reporting, hard-boiled without being cynical.

In the 1930s many people compared Hammett to Hemingway, often suggesting Hammett was there first with hard-boiled prose. This was unfair to Hemingway, because *In Our Time* is crafted with a bare purity that has rarely been matched. Hemingway attributed that purity to learning "cable-ese," the pared-down prose necessary to save on the cost of wiring his reporting back to the paper at home. But neither writer has the raw, hard-boiled quality of Paul Cain's *Fast One* or Raoul Whitfield's *Green Ice*. Look elsewhere in Hemingway or at some of Hammett and you'll find prose crafted in an almost romantic manner, because they refuse to submit completely to cynicism; they've seen too much of reality for that.

Connelly decided to become a crime writer after seeing Robert Altman's cynical version of *The Long Goodbye* and turning to Chandler's novels, which he devoured one by one. At the University of Florida, he studied creative writing with the novelist Harry Crews. Although he claims Crews' lifestyle and his success as a writer were more of an influence than his style, I see elements of Crews' darkness, somewhere between Southern gothic and theater of the absurd, in Connelly's fiction. I also see, in Harry Bosch, a very Crewsian figure, out of place in his world, and stretched to breaking point trying to make himself fit.

Bosch is the catalyst that allows Connelly to perform the trick of turning reality into fiction. The art of writing good hard-boiled prose requires a certain detachment, the ability to not let the runny emotional yolk of a story break free.

But it doesn't have to be boiled within the shell. The closest comparison I can make in crime fiction is with Ross MacDonald, whose Lew Archer is an observer of social change, almost a reporter, and whose prose brings the reader a clear perspective on what Archer sees, freed of cynicism and ornamentation.

This is exactly the sense in which I think of Michael

Connelly as a hard-boiled writer, and one of the most successful. He has been able to achieve that detachment without losing the emotional center, without sacrificing empathy. He is able to sustain a paradoxical sense of distance and involvement in his fiction — like a reporter, sharing the experience of cops without becoming one himself, balancing the grief of victims, the nature of victimizers, the frustrations of cops. He learned to do it in the pieces collected here.

PERHAPS YOU NOTICED I began this essay by saying Michael Connelly *is* a reporter. Not was a reporter. Is.

The would-be novelist stuck in a career as a newsman is an old cliché. I don't see Michael ever being stuck. I don't know if he went to his first crime scene and gathered his notes with the idea of finding material for his books. You will certainly see in these stories the raw materials — the crimes, the criminals, the cops and the city — that make up his fiction. But what these pieces do show is that Connelly was a hell of a good reporter. And that being a hell of a good reporter was a great start for becoming a hell of a good novelist.

MICHAEL CARLSON was born in New Haven, Connecticut, and lives in London with his wife and son. He has written about Michael Connelly for the *Spectator, Daily*

Telegraph, Financial Times, Perth (Australia) *Sunday Times, Shots* and *Crime Time,* where he also edits the film section. His studies of the directors Sergio Leone, Clint Eastwood and Oliver Stone were published in the Pocket Essentials series.

ACKNOWLEDGMENTS

The stories contained in this collection all carried the byline of Michael Connelly but without exception they were all labored over by numerous editors, copyeditors and fellow reporters. It is impossible to write a newspaper or magazine story without the input of many. I wish to thank all of those who helped make these stories fit to print.

I also wish to thank Michael Pietsch, Asya Muchnick and Pamela Marshall for their more recent work in making the stories suitable for reprinting here. And last but not least, special thanks to Steven Vascik of SCV Publications for first gathering and publishing this collection.

PERMISSIONS

ROOKIE OFFICER DIES IN STRUGGLE FOR GUN

DEATH FOR DEATH

1,000 ATTEND RITES FOR SLAIN ROOKIE OFFICER

4 MEN ARRESTED IN LAKE VIEW TERRACE
QUADRUPLE KILLING

DRUG RING KINGPIN CALLS THE SHOTS FROM
PRISON, POLICE SAY

AMBUSH SHOOTING

WHO SHOT VIC WEISS?

'COTTON CLUB' CASE LED TO ARREST IN '84 SLAYING
OF PROSTITUTE

SUSPECT REMAINS AT LARGE ALMOST 2 YEARS
AFTER HIS FATHER'S SLAYING

MURDER OF KANAN HEIR REMAINS A MYSTERY

POLICE SURVEILLANCE UNIT KILLS 3 ROBBERY
SUSPECTS

MICHAEL BRYANT'S DOUBLE LIFE

NEPHEW IDENTIFIED AS SOLE SUSPECT IN KANAN KILLING

DAUGHTER SAYS FATHER, WIFE HE'S ACCUSED OF KILLING HAD ARGUED

TRIAL ORDERED FOR MAN ACCUSED OF KILLING WIFE, BURYING HER IN YARD

MAN CHARGED IN 1982 DEATH ALLEGES POLICE VENDETTA

CHARGES WILL NOT BE FILED IN KANAN CASE

SELF-PROMOTING 'CONTRACT KILLER' ENTERS PLEA TO KILLING WIFE IN '85

MURDER SUSPECT SEEKS TO CLEAR NAME WITH LAWSUITS

WIFE STILL A SUSPECT IN HUSBAND'S DEATH AFTER LOSING SUIT

KILLING OF SPOUSE PUTS AN END TO MAN'S DOUBLE LIFE

ATTORNEY CALLS SPECIAL LAPD SQUAD 'ASSASSINS'
AS CIVIL RIGHTS TRIAL OPENS

FBI PROBES SLAYING OF ROBBERS BY LAPD

CHRISTOPHER REPORT: IT CUTS BOTH WAYS

L.A. DETECTIVE TELLS DETAILS OF FATAL SHOOTING

GATES WANTS TO BE 'JUDGE, JURY, EXECUTIONER,'
LAWYER SAYS

COUNCIL SUED OVER FATAL POLICE SHOOTING

MASSIVE DRUG, MURDER CASE INCHES ITS WAY
TOWARD TRIAL

VALLEY POLICE PUZZLE OVER MAN'S DEATH DURING
RIOTS

ATTORNEYS AWARDED FEE OF $378,000 IN BRUTALITY
SUIT

ABOUT THE AUTHOR

MICHAEL CONNELLY is a former journalist and the author of the bestselling series of Harry Bosch novels, including *Echo Park* and *The Closers,* along with the bestselling novels *The Lincoln Lawyer, Chasing the Dime, Void Moon, Blood Work,* and *The Poet.* Connelly has won numerous awards for his journalism and novels, including an Edgar Award. He is the former president of Mystery Writers of America.